Happy Student

Happy Student

The Practical Guide to Functional Behavior Assessment and Behavior Intervention Planning

Jenna Sage

ROWMAN & LITTLEFIELD
Lanham • Boulder • New York • London

Published by Rowman & Littlefield
A wholly owned subsidiary of The Rowman & Littlefield Publishing Group, Inc.
4501 Forbes Boulevard, Suite 200, Lanham, Maryland 20706
www.rowman.com

6 Tinworth Street, London SE11 5AL

British Library Cataloguing in Publication Information Available

Library of Congress Cataloging-in-Publication Data Available

Includes bibliographic references and index.
ISBN 9781475836578 (cloth : alk. paper)
ISBN 9781475836585 (pbk. : alk. paper)
ISBN 9781475836592 (Electronic)

♾™ The paper used in this publication meets the minimum requirements of
American National Standard for Information Sciences—Permanence of Paper
for Printed Library Materials, ANSI/NISO Z39.48-1992.

Printed in the United States of America

Contents

Introduction

FIRST THINGS FIRST

This book is likely in your hands right now because you have had some experience with Functional Behavioral Assessments and Behavior Intervention Plans (FBA/BIP). You are probably a teacher, an administrator, a parent, a behavior analyst, school support staff, or maybe even a student yourself. You have probably even leafed through the dense pages of manuals and textbooks on FBAs and BIPs.

First things first, this is not a manual; this book is not intended to teach you step by step how to do an FBA or BIP. This book will provide the tips and tricks to this process. This book will give you some practical strategies. This book is going to *guide* you through the process. And this is very intentional. There are hundreds of books available with the step-by-step directions, but you are holding this book in your hands because you want the *practical strategies*. You want to learn more about the why. You want pragmatic, time efficient, utilitarian, nitty-gritty.

I know because I have been there; I have been in your shoes. I'm an educator first. I understand that oftentimes someone comes into the classroom from "the outside" and gives advice on how to address challenging behavior and creates a plan that doesn't meet the needs of the classroom or the teacher. I have seen too many teachers wash their hands of behavior analysis and the FBA/BIP process because they weren't part of the planning.

I'm also a Board Certified Behavior Analyst (BCBA); I have worked with thousands of students, teachers, families, administrators, school psychologists, social workers, paraprofessionals, and more to better understand the FBA/BIP process. Most of the time, they expressed that they have tried "that behavior analysis stuff" and it hasn't worked. And it probably didn't.

The goal of this book is not only to ensure that you are included as part of the planning but also to provide you with the practical skills to be the planner, to develop plans that accomplish the most important goal, which is to increase the quality of life for a student with challenging behavior and everyone in the classroom experiencing the challenging behavior . . . including you.

Each chapter is arranged to include a blank chart at the beginning of the chapter. This is the focus area for the chapter and the corresponding component of a functional behavioral assessment and behavior intervention plan. The end of each chapter will have a series of reflection questions for you to go deeper with your learning. The chapters also include a completed chart to provide an example of how to carry the information from the chapter over into the assessment and plan. There are appendices with the completed plans as well so you can see the full process for two example students.

INGREDIENTS OF ALPHABET SOUP

In this fast-paced, acronym-filled world of education it can often feel like you are floating in the broth of alphabet soup. There are so many new terms, acronyms, and practices each year that it can be difficult to manage the menagerie. It can often feel like it requires a practice in deciphering hieroglyphs or translating a foreign language.

If your administrator asked you to work with the MDT to gather the CBMs for the FBA before the IEP meeting for the student with EBD to determine the DRA for the BIP, would you know where to start? It can seem intimidating, but this book will help you to decode the tangle of acronyms and make the process of understanding student behavior much less intimidating.

(For your reference, here's the translation for that sentence: *Work with the Multi-Disciplinary Team (MDT) to gather the Curriculum-Based Measures (CBM) for the Functional Behavior Assessment (FBA) before the Individual Education Plan (IEP) meeting for the student with Emotional Behavioral Disability (EBD) to determine the Differential Reinforcement of Alternative (DRA) behavior for the Behavior Intervention Plan (BIP).*)

WHICH RECIPE WILL WORK FOR ME?

How do you know what to do and when? There are several ways to consider moving through the FBA and BIP process. Consider MTSS, described in table 0.1. The FBA, BIP, and WA can all be thought of as a tiered system of support.

Table 0.1. Common Terms Used in the Functional Behavior Process

ABA	Applied Behavior Analysis	Scientific application of behavioral principles to applied settings
BIP	Behavior Intervention Plan	Implementation plan developed after conducting a functional behavioral assessment
FBA	Functional Behavior Assessment (Analysis)	Assessment: observation and assessment process to better understand the function of behavior Analysis: experimental conditions created to evaluate the function of behavior
MDT	Multi-Disciplinary Team	Team of interdisciplinary school-based professionals working together to problem solve (often includes family member[s])
MTSS	Multi-Tiered Systems of Support	Triaged system of supports designed to ensure that *all* students receive core instruction, *some* students receive additional supports plus the core instruction, and *a few* students receive intense/individualized supports plus the core and support instruction (academic and behavior instruction)
PBIS	Positive Behavior Interventions and Supports	System of behavioral MTSS designed specifically to address school-wide, classroom, group, and individual student needs
PSP	Problem-Solving Process	Four- to eight-step process to better understand challenging behavior or situations
RtI	Response to Intervention	Assessment/evaluation process to better understand how a student is responding to the implementation of an intervention or plan
WA	Wrap Around	Multi-disciplinary team consisting of school, family, and community supports working together to problem solve

First, although often not seen in this sequence, is the Behavior Intervention Plan. Why would this be first when it is most commonly linked to the FBA? Because there are often times when you as the classroom teacher or behavior support person already have a very good understanding of the student and what may be maintaining the challenging behavior. Because of this, there may be no need to conduct the functional assessment. This can only be done when it is clear what the possible function may be. The team may be able to dive directly into the creation of a behavior plan.

For minor or less serious challenging behaviors (talking out of turn, wandering around the classroom, time off task, etc.), it may be best to begin by developing a plan aligned to the team's hypothesized function of behavior. In chapter 5, you'll learn much more about the hypothesized function and will be better prepared to know if you can start addressing challenging behavior with a BIP and without doing a formal FBA first.

In some cases, it may not be clear why the student is engaging in the challenging behavior. This is when the team should consider an FBA. This assessment process is what helps to hypothesize the function of behavior and then develop a BIP based on the findings. This process takes more time and requires more intensified observation and data collection.

It may seem counterintuitive to begin with the process that requires more time when a child is engaging in serious, aggressive, or complicated behaviors, but it is also more ethically sound. Consider that the FBA process, while complex and lengthy, allows for a deeper understanding of the behavior, and therefore a more precise plan can be created.

If a behavior analyst is involved in the process, he or she may recommend creating an experimental design to determine the function of behavior. This is the only stage during which the function is determined due to testing all of the possible functions and not just hypothesized. During an FBA (Functional Behavioral *Analysis*),[1] a series of different arrangements will be created to observe the student's response to functional scenarios. This is rarely done in the applied school settings because it is difficult to replicate real-world, busy, fast-paced classrooms. Some districts and schools may use the terms "analysis" and "assessment" interchangeably; however, there is an important distinction. The analysis tests the hypothesized function, and the assessment only uses the hypothesized function.

There are also times when the MDT does not have sufficient data and information to build a strong BIP from the assessment process or when the FBA implementation needs an additional layer. This is when a Wrap Around[2] process may be considered. Wrap Around brings in members of the student's family and community (church, agency affiliation, foster or state representation, legal representation, little league coach, etc.) to help the student to develop the plan and participate in the creation and adjustment of plan specifics. In this case, the student is more directly involved in the development of his or her plan and is able to participate in the creation and adjustment of plan specifics.

This book is organized to lead a teacher, team, or family member through an FBA and develop an aligned BIP. It is recommended that the book be read in its entirety first. Once there is an understanding of how the FBA and BIP work together, then the MDT could focus on certain areas like data col-

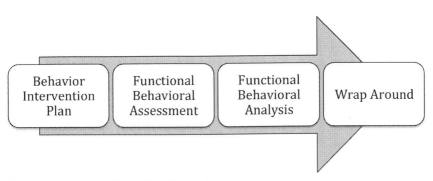

Figure 0.1. Layers of Behavioral Support

lection or just the BIP based on the needs of the student. The beginning of each chapter has a sample of the focus component area of the FBA or BIP. The end of each chapter has a completed component of the FBA or BIP as an example. The example FBA/BIPs can also be found in the appendices for a quick reference.

SHIPPING AND RECEIVING

All too often what has been experienced when consulting and working through the FBA/BIP process in school settings is the misnomer that the process is intended to justify the movement of a student from a less restrictive setting to a more restrictive setting. In other words, it is a shipping and receiving document intended to move a student from one classroom to another or from one school to another. This is heartbreaking.

While much of the work is viewed as compliance driven—a process of checking off that each step was completed—instead the end goal should *always* be a happy, successful student. At times the result may be that the student requires more support than could be afforded in a general education classroom or with typically developing peers; however, the end goal is not the placement of the student but *how* (that is, quality of life) the student is.

A student with challenging behavior may already have plans and goals that have been created. It is likely that if the behavior has been occurring for a length of time or has impacted the student's ability to function successfully in the classroom, intensive plans have been attempted. The goal of the functional behavioral assessment is not to override what has been done previously or to take the place of any current or successful strategies. The FBA process is designed to ensure that the plans that are in place are aligned with the function of the behavior so that there is greater likelihood of success.

Behavior Agreement		
Teacher: Student: Date:		

I _____ agree to do the following:
- Arrive to class on time.
- Have my materials ready.
- Follow instructions the first time given.

I understand the consequences for not meeting the above will be:
- I will lose the privilege of listening to music during breaks.

I will know I have been successful when:
- I have arrived on time, been ready, and followed instructions for one week.

For following the agreement I will earn:
- The ability to listen to music during independent work time in the classroom for one period.

Teacher Signature:	Student Signature:	Administrator Signature:
Date:	Date:	Date:

Figure 0.2.   Behavior Agreement

In many cases previous plans have been created without the assessment of the function of behavior. A student may have a less formal plan like a behavior agreement or contract. A behavior agreement is a short-term plan created between the teacher and the student. It typically defines the challenging behavior, outlines several steps to decrease the behavior, determines consequences for not following the steps, and creates a goal or criteria to meet for success. This can be helpful for minor behaviors.

Some students may already have a more intensive plan in place to address behavior or academic success. The most common plan is an Individual Education Plan (IEP). An IEP is created when a student meets the state and federal criteria for special education services. These plans have strict governance based on legislative criteria and may address academic and behavioral challenges.

The FBA process can occur prior to a student being found eligible for special education services or after. Ideally, the FBA is done prior with the goal of eliminating the need for more intensive supports. This is often done through a Response to Intervention (RtI) framework. An RtI framework is designed to match the intensity of intervention need. The first level or tier of support is what every student receives. In academics this is typically the core content. In behavior, this is often the basic classroom management system.

If a student or group of students is not successful with that initial level of support, another layer is added on to provide more intensive teaching. In academics this may be small group instruction in a particular subject area or with a specific skill (for example, a small group focused on multiplying double digits or a small group that receives additional time to practice reading strategies). In behavior this may also be small group instruction. The instruction for behavior may be aimed at addressing specific social skills (for example, a small group that is learning how to initiate a conversation with a peer or how to use calming techniques when frustrated). The important part is that the students are intentionally grouped based on a similar skill and the level of intensity matches the need.

For students that require more practice, more time is allotted for that practice. If that process of grouping and matching the level of intensity is not successful, an additional layer may be added to provide more individualized supports. This level of support is intended for severe challenges in academics and/or behavior. This level of support is also layered on top of the other layers. In other words, if a student is significantly below grade level in reading, he or she receives the core reading content, plus small group reading intervention, plus individual reading support. For behavior, a student who experiences significant challenging behavior receives the supports of the classroom management system, additional small group instruction in social skills, plus individual intervention specific for that student.

Most often that individual level of support is the behavior plan that is developed from the FBA. When you develop an FBA, you are creating an individualized behavior plan to address a specific skill deficit for the student. If you have gotten to this point and feel that there could be additional layers of support done before an individualized plan, that is fine. You can go back and assess the classroom management system to determine if it meets the needs of most students and is based on best practices. You can go back and ensure that some small group instruction has taken place or organize some small group supports. The aim of any process is to attain the goal by creating the greatest level of success with minimal expenditure of time and resources.

THE END IN MIND

If the team, teacher, administrator, or support personnel are able to always advocate for the goal of a happy quality of life, then the process will fall into place. Consider this proverb from *Thich Nhat Hanh*:

> *When you plant lettuce, if it does not grow well, you don't blame the lettuce. You look for reasons it is not doing well. It may need fertilizer, or more water, or*

less sun. You never blame the lettuce. Yet if we have problems with our friends or family, we blame the other person. But if we know how to take care of them, they will grow well, like the lettuce. Blaming has no positive effect at all, nor does trying to persuade using reason and argument. That is my experience. No blame, no reasoning, no argument, just understanding. If you understand, and you show that you understand, you can love, and the situation will change.

The process of understanding the function of behavior is not about blame or what the student should do better or different. The process is about understanding, loving, and seeing positive change.

NOTES

1. John O. Cooper, Timothy E. Heron, and William L. Heward, *Applied Behavior Analysis* (Upper Saddle River, NJ: Pearson/Merrill-Prentice Hall, 2007).
2. https://www.pbis.org/school/tertiary-level/wraparound.

Part I

FUNCTIONAL
BEHAVIOR ASSESSMENT

Chapter One

Do You See What I See?

Describing and Defining the Target Behavior

Remember: everyone in the classroom has a story that leads to misbehavior or defiance. Nine times out of ten, the story behind the misbehavior won't make you angry. It will break your heart.

—*Annette Breaux*

Describing and defining the target behavior is an essential component in the overall problem-solving process.[1] The only way to create a viable and effective Behavior Intervention Plan is to ensure that we are addressing the correct target behavior, the "what" of the problem-solving process. All too often, teams and individuals quickly begin to hypothesize the "why" without clearly defining the "what." Not having the "what" leads to ineffective plans, wasted time and energy, and a belief that the functional assessment process for the behavior change process is unproductive.

Table 1.1. Target Behavior

Description of the Target Behavior (as described and/or observed by classroom staff)
Operational Definition of Target Behavior (should include all elements necessary)

3

The "what" begins with operationally defining the challenging behavior. The team or classroom teacher has already identified that some behavior is impeding learning or interfering with the daily routine. Frequently the conversation sounds similar to this: *"Sonya is constantly interrupting instruction. She bounces in her seat all day long, if she can even stay in it. She's also been hitting another child during recess lately. I can't get any teaching done with her in the classroom."* Or, *"Murray is always mouthing off in class. He thinks he's the class clown. Every time I am instructing he has something smart to say. I can't keep him in my class if he's always going to be disrespectful."*

Sound familiar? There are some key words that we can pick up on in the two scenarios. Some of the terms will help us to define the "what" and some of the words will help us later with the assessment to determine the "how often."

TEXTBOX 1.1.
Key Terms

What are some key terms that you feel would help us to describe and define the behavior?

IS IT A BEHAVIOR?

One of the seminal concepts in Applied Behavior Analysis (ABA) is what most practitioners refer to as the Dead Man Test or the Potato Test. The concept is intended to help you think in observable and measurable terms. In other words, if a dead man or a potato can do it, it isn't a behavior. Why is this important? In order to change behavior, we have to have behavior. A sound behavioral definition is built on something that can be seen, clearly observed, quantified, and measured.

One of the most commonly used behavioral terms in education is "noncompliance." This is a nebulous term. It could mean hundreds of things depending on who is asked. It also alludes to a lack of behavior. Can a potato be noncompliant? When a potato is asked to peel itself does it comply? Of course not!

Take a moment to think about how you would define noncompliance. What has it looked like in classrooms that you have observed? How have other educators described it to you?

A viable definition of a student who is being noncompliant would instead describe the *behaviors* that the child *is* engaging in. The student may be talking out of turn, walking out of line, wandering in the classroom, doodling in a textbook, wearing his or her sweatshirt hood over his or her eyes, etc.

The goal is to understand the challenging behavior in enough detail that when observing, it is clear what behavior to look for. That begins with the operational definition. An operational definition has multiple parts. The definition should include

- a title or brief description of the behavior,
- the topography (physical movements involved) of the behavior,
- the hypothesized frequency of the behavior,
- the hypothesized length or duration of the behavior, and
- a description of the behavior's intensity.

Let's look at Sonya's scenario again. *"Sonya is constantly interrupting instruction. She bounces in her seat all day long, if she can even stay in it. She's even been hitting another child during recess lately. I can't get any teaching done with her in the classroom."* This time, several key words were underlined. Were they the same words that you homed in on?

The underlined words give clues to the challenging behaviors that are being seen in the classroom. In this case, there are several behaviors that appear to be impacting Sonya's success. When this occurs, it may be necessary to prioritize behaviors.

An FBA that is written with the goal of ameliorating multiple behaviors at once is going to be more intensive and more difficult to create a BIP. So the MDT may need to triage the plans and prioritize the most impactful behavior. This requires that the team determine what behavior has the most impact on the child's quality of life and academic success or requires the most immediate response.

There are four phrases or keywords underlined for Sonya. Which behavior should the MDT address? Where should the team focus?

As a classroom teacher, the most common instinct is to go with the behavior(s) that impact academic success the most or is the most frustrating. *All too often, the target behavior is chosen based on the preference of the person feeling challenged by the behavior rather than determining the behavior based on the greatest need of the child.* As a classroom teacher, the desire may be to focus on the interrupting based on the frequency of its occurrence. It feels as though this behavior is having the most significant impact in the classroom and impeding Sonya's academic success. This may be the case.

However, hitting other children is not an acceptable behavior under any circumstances. Physical aggression, if it is present, should almost always be prioritized, even if it is not happening regularly or as often as the other behaviors. An effective FBA and BIP can quickly address the most challenging behavior, in this case hitting, and then be adjusted later to address the other behaviors of concern. Emergency room doctors have to quickly and efficiently determine what injuries require the most immediate attention and care. It does not mean that they forgo treating the other wounds. It means that they prioritize based on need. The FBA/BIP process also requires that prioritization.

Now that it has been identified that the focus of the current assessment will be hitting, an operational definition can be created. The first step in that definition is to describe the behavior. In this case, hitting is a fairly easy description and fairly universally understood.

What Does the Behavior Look Like?

Next is describing the topography of the behavior. "Topography"[2] is a term that originates in map making and studying the earth's shapes and features. The process is very similar when it comes to behavior. When creating an operational definition, it is necessary to describe the shape and features of the behavior.

For Sonya, the behavior is hitting. "Hitting" may seem like a simple term. It may seem as though creating a definition of what a hit looks like, sounds like, and feels like would be easy. But could that information all be described so that a person sitting across the room could understand the same features? That is the ultimate goal. A good operational definition will be clear to anyone reading it. It will be an objective and nonemotional description of the behavior. It will describe the behavior well enough that a stranger could identify and count the same behavior the same number of times.

An example of the topography of hitting may include making physical contact with a person or object using an open hand, closed fist, or any or all parts of the hand connecting with the person or object. The hitting may or may not leave a mark. The hitting may also include other parts of the arm connecting with the person or object.

As a stranger, would it be clear when to tally a hit when observing Sonya? It may seem excessive to include so much detail in a description of challenging behavior; however, remember that the intent is that there is a clear picture of the "what" so that when understanding the "why" and "what to do" there is a solid foundation to build on. This definition will also ensure that accurate data are able to be collected and analyzed to make the best decisions for the behavior change process.

Building on What Is Known

The next part of the definition involves some guesswork. It may be the case that prior data have been collected before the behavioral definition creation and be based on the assumed target behavior. Those data may not be accurate or reflect this updated definition, however, any data or information will help to determine when and how to collect additional data.

Let's look at the teacher's description of the challenging behavior again. *"Sonya is constantly <u>interrupting</u> instruction. She <u>bounces in her seat</u> all day long, if she can even <u>stay in it</u>. She's even been <u>hitting</u> another child during recess lately. I can't get any teaching done with her in the classroom."* Unfortunately, this description does not give us much to go on regarding the frequency, duration, or intensity. The frequency equates to how often the behavior may occur. The duration is for how long the behavior may be occurring. Does it last for seconds, minutes, or hours continuously? The intensity is the degree to which it may have an impact. All of which are described in greater detail in chapter 4.

In Sonya's case, it is clearer where it happens. It may be necessary to ask some additional members of the MDT to gain a clearer picture on some of the aspects of the behavior. Keep in mind that at this point hypothesized information is okay. Additional data will be taken later and throughout the FBA/BIP process to gather more detailed information.

Hypothesizing information about Sonya's hitting behavior, imagine that it occurs up to two times during the twenty-minute recess and can happen up to three days a week. The hitting does not leave a mark but does leave the other child upset. The behavior does not last more than a second or two at a time.

Based on all of the information present, an operational definition can be built and would likely look like:

Sonya's hitting behavior is defined as a hit that makes physical contact with a person or object using an open hand, closed fist, or any or all parts of the hand connecting with the person or object. The hitting may or may not leave a mark. The hitting may also include other parts of the arm connecting with the person or object. The hitting behavior occurs nearly six times per week during recess. The hitting does not leave a mark on the other person and each hit lasts only a second or two.

OPERATIONALIZING THE BEHAVIOR

Taking a look at Murray's scenario, create an operational definition that includes all of the necessary components: *"Murray is always <u>mouthing off</u> in class. He thinks he's the <u>class clown</u>. Every time I am instructing he has something smart to say. I can't keep him in my class if he's always going to be disrespectful."* Several of the key words describing the challenging behavior are underlined to assist.

The first step would be to describe "mouthing off." This is a behavior that may mean very different things to different people. The variance in the definition may depend on a person's tolerance level, beliefs, culture, and background, etc. A term like "mouthing off" needs a clear and clean operational definition.

The scenario also uses terms like "always" and "every time." Those may give the MDT a clue to hypothesize the frequency, duration, and intensity. However, it is cautioned that anytime the terms "always" and "every time" are used, they are likely an exaggeration of the actual frequency or intensity. While it may feel like always, there are typically times that it occurs more or less; there may be variables that impact the number of times the behavior occurs and additional information that can help to delineate the frequency.

Later in the process it will be necessary to collect data on the target behavior. If it occurs "always," data will need to be collected 100 percent of the time. That can create a resource and time challenge for the classroom teacher. If the MDT can better define how much and how often, a more precise data collection system can be created, including pinpointing when to collect the data.

In Murray's case, presume that the behavior is occurring up to fifteen times during a fifty-minute period. The behavior is interrupting instruction and interfering with the learning of others. The vocalizations are loud enough to be heard across the classroom; they are above a whisper level (for example, topography).

The operational definition may look something like this:

Murray's mouthing off behavior is defined as vocalizations that are unrelated to instruction or activities. Vocalizations may be inappropriate based on school rules and policies, may include threats or harmful terms. Vocalizations may or may not be directly addressed to another student or staff member. Vocalizations occur up to fifteen times during a fifty-minute class period and are above a whisper level. Vocalizations can be heard throughout the classroom environment.

Creating operational definitions takes practice. It requires that the MDT remove judgment and emotion and look at the behavior objectively. It may be helpful to have a "stranger" to the behavior read the definition and determine if it is clear and easy to identify the challenging behavior. Just remember to remove any personal or identifiable information first to ensure confidentiality. A good definition should pass both the Dead Man/Potato Test, and the Stranger Test.

The next step in the FBA process will be to take a deeper look into understanding the target behavior. In this chapter a clear definition was created to ensure that the MDT and all stakeholders could identify the challenging behavior. The next chapter will examine where the behavior is most and least likely to occur, as well as interview stakeholders and conduct a records review.

REFLECTION QUESTIONS

1. What would an operational definition of a *tantrum* look like?
2. What questions would you ask the classroom teacher to determine more information about the frequency, duration, and intensity of a behavior?
3. Does the behavior of "not following directions" pass the Dead Man Test or the Potato Test? Why or why not? How could the behavior be described differently?

Table 1.2. Completed Target Behavior

Description of the Target Behavior (as described and/or observed by classroom staff) Hitting other students, aggression, not playing with others
Operational Definition of Target Behavior (should include all elements necessary) Sonya's hitting behavior is defined as a hit that makes physical contact with a person or object using an open hand, closed fist, or any or all parts of the hand connecting with the person or object. The hitting may or may not leave a mark. The hitting may also include other parts of the arm connecting with the person or object. The hitting behavior occurs nearly six times per week during recess. The hitting does not leave a mark on the other person and each hit lasts only a second or two.

NOTES

1. R. C. Martella, J. Ron Nelson, N. E. Marchand-Martella, and M. O'Reilly, *Comprehensive Behavior Management: Individualized, Classroom, and Schoolwide Approaches* (Thousand Oaks, CA: SAGE Publications Inc., 2012).

2. John O. Cooper, Timothy E. Heron, and William L. Heward, *Applied Behavior Analysis* (Upper Saddle River, NJ: Pearson/Merrill-Prentice Hall, 2007).

Chapter Two

Asking the Right Questions

Understanding the Target Behavior

When we encounter a challenging student, we have a choice. To ruminate about their impact on you and your class, or to reflect on what you can learn about them or your own practice from their behaviors.

—*TIPBS.com*

Now that you have determined the "what" of the behavior—the operational definition—you can begin to piece together other parts of the behavior puzzle that will help to eventually create a behavior plan. The next step is digging a bit deeper into the "where" and identifying who else can provide additional information. Results from interviews will help to understand "where" to collect data and the accuracy of the target behavior definition.

Let's look at the description of Sonya's behavior again. *"Sonya is constantly interrupting instruction. She bounces in her seat all day long, if she can even stay in it. She's even been hitting another child during recess lately. I can't get any teaching done with her in the classroom."* This same scenario can be used to gather clues about where the behavior is occurring most often and whom else we may want to gather more details from.

From the teacher's description, the behavior appears to occur in the classroom and during recess. In this case, it is clear. But what if you didn't have enough information or the behavior occurred *everywhere*? Sometimes descriptions are too vague or too detailed. In those cases, observations of the behavior will need to occur. It does not have to be formal, but the observations can be several hours or up to a day or two shadowing the student to observe where the behavior occurs most and least throughout the day. Approximations of how many times the behavior occurs across locations may be necessary. That information will help to pinpoint an effective data collection system later in the process.

Table 2.1. Settings and Interviews

Setting(s) in which the Target Behavior occurs most often (as described and/or observed by classroom staff)	☐ Classroom ☐ Hallway ☐ Specials/Electives ☐ Playground/Parking Lot ☐ Gym ☐ Cafeteria ☐ Office Areas ☐ Bus/Transportation ☐ Transitions (between activities, between subject areas, between classes, etc.) ☐ Unknown ☐ Other: describe
Anecdotal Report	Teacher Interview: Student Interview: Parent Interview: Other:

Remember from chapter 1, *"in the classroom"* may not provide enough details for us to create an effective and meaningful data collection system. Who else could be asked for more details about the *where*? Who else interacts with Sonya enough to help specify locations?

BUILDING AN INTERVIEW

The first thing to do is to ask the classroom teacher for more details. If you are the classroom teacher, you can also do a self-interview. The classroom teacher is the person that spends the majority of time with the student. Studies[1] across a variety of research topics have shown that teachers are fairly accurate in understanding the needs of the students in their classrooms. The important part is gathering the right kind of information. If there are not specific interview questions, then responses may continue to be vague or provide nondescript evidence.

The interview should help to build the rest of the FBA components, including where to observe and collect data, how to concisely summarize the target behavior, and how to develop a hypothesis for why the behavior is occurring. The interview questions should also allow the interviewee to share what has worked and not worked in the past. Oftentimes, when creating a behavior plan with a teacher, there will be apprehension because he or she has likely already implemented a variety of strategies and interventions to try to decrease or stop the challenging behavior.

The difference is that teachers typically haven't collected the *right* data nor have they created the hypothesis for the "why," the function of the behavior. So they have really been throwing the pot of noodles at the wall and seeing if any of the noodles stick, metaphorically speaking. Teachers will often feel fatigued with trying new interventions because they feel they have exhausted all of their options. And that may be the case. If you know what has worked and hasn't worked in the past, you can build on successful strategies and fine tune them so they are more aligned to the function of the behavior and more easily implemented in the classroom. In other words, you can help to find just the right al dente noodle.

To find that noodle, we have to find the right questions. Consider again what we already know from the description. *"Sonya is constantly interrupting instruction. She bounces in her seat all day long, if she can even stay in it. She's even been hitting another child during recess lately. I can't get any teaching done with her in the classroom."*

Again, behavior detective, there are some great clues to help build interview questions from. Different pieces of information are underlined here that can be used to dive deeper into the behavior of concern. Also consider the fact that the teacher is still likely concerned about the other behaviors even though the plan is going to focus on the hitting behavior. It is important to honor the teacher's concerns around those other behaviors and that those behaviors will also be addressed if possible. Here are some sample questions.

- How often do you believe, or have you observed, the hitting behavior occurring?
- Does the hitting only occur during recess or has it been reported or observed in other locations?
- What happens right after the hitting? How do adults respond? How do the other students and the victim respond?
- What strategies have been tried to stop the hitting?
- How do you feel those strategies have worked?
- Are there other behaviors that you are concerned about?
- Where do those most often and least often occur?
- What strategies have been tried to decrease those behaviors?
- What has worked and not worked?
- Is there any other information that you feel would help to create a plan that you will be implementing?

These questions should help to build a stronger foundation of what is happening and why it may be happening. Let's look at some possible responses to those questions for Sonya and see if any clues can be gathered.

- How often do you believe, or have you observed, the hitting behavior occurring? *I have seen hitting several times on the playground, but I have heard other students mention that they have seen her hit friends. My partner teacher also mentioned one day that she had seen Sonya lash out at a classmate.*
- Does hitting only occur during recess or has it been reported or observed in other locations? *I think it happens during times or in places where there is less structure. I see other behaviors in the classroom during transitions and when all the students are together it can be chaotic and overwhelming. It is loud and a bit overstimulating. My partner teacher mentioned that she saw Sonya hit another student in the hallway.*
- What happens right after the hitting? How do adults respond? How do the other students and the victim respond? *In the instances that I have seen the hitting, the student that was hit began crying and yelling, the other students around Sonya got mad at her and told her to stop, and the adult that was monitoring during recess immediately went over and talked to Sonya about how hitting is bad and made her apologize. I don't have much information about the other instances. My partner teacher might be able to share details of what she saw.*
- What strategies have been tried to stop the hitting? *Well, after Sonya has hit, she has had to apologize, she has been removed from the situation, she has lost privileges, and she has gotten a phone call home.*
- How do you feel those have worked? *I'm not sure. The apology made the other student feel better temporarily. But I think that Sonya continues to become more aggressive. While she isn't hitting students in the classroom that I have seen, she has been more confrontational, argumentative, and emotional. I can see her physically lashing out at students in the classroom if something isn't done.*
- Are there other behaviors that you are concerned about? *Hitting is pretty extreme, but she also is very disruptive in the class. She wanders around the classroom, she fidgets a lot, and she has a hard time sitting still. And, like I mentioned, she has become more emotional, which can also be disruptive.*
- Where do those most often and least often occur? *Well, it happens in the classroom, but the more I think about it, it starts after we have transitions. When we move from one activity to the next. That is probably most often. Sometimes it happens when the students are doing independent work. She will try to get me to spend more time with her.*

- What strategies have been tried to decrease those behaviors? *I feel like I've tried everything. I have moved her seat. I have tried to comfort her. I have used time out, a lot. She has lost privileges. Most often, I think I try to redirect her and get her to refocus. I noticed that when I work with her more one on one, she seems fine.*
- What has worked and not worked? *Most of the strategies I described really haven't made it better and I can't work with her one on one all day long. The other students need me too. The only other thing that has worked in the past was going to visit her favorite specials teacher Mrs. Davidson. She loves her! I had her go there one day when she couldn't handle being in my class anymore and she came back after forty-five minutes like a different child.*
- Is there any other information that you feel would help to create a plan that you will be implementing? *I just know that I'm exhausted. It is hard trying to focus on Sonya and her needs while also helping everyone else. I need to be able to teach and I most certainly don't want other students to be fearful or scared that they'll be hit or hurt. I've already had two other parents contact me with their concerns.*

Do the interview responses help to understand the "what" and "where" better? You could even interview the partner teacher for more information. While you don't want to spend a great deal of time interviewing, finding out a few details directly from sources that have observed the challenging behavior can be very helpful.

ASKING THE STUDENT

If the student is developmentally able to respond to interview questions, you can ask him or her directly what he or she feels is happening. Even young students have a keen sense of self-awareness and are often able to articulate their concerns, challenges, goals, and strategies. There is no right or wrong when it comes to determining if the student should be interviewed. The best thing is to create three to five simple questions to ask, and if the student is responsive, great. If his or she is not responsive or if the questioning evokes the challenging behavior(s), then stop the interview and continue with the other steps in the FBA process.

It is recommended to let the student know, especially if he or she is older, that the information can remain confidential unless it is dangerous or harmful, and in that case, someone qualified will need to be notified to provide the necessary supports. It may not be anticipated, but students of all developmental ages and stages often overshare information during this process. They will divulge a great deal of information, often because not many people have taken the time to ask them directly what is happening. The student interview is not required, but when it can be completed, it is often helpful.

Here are some sample student questions. If the student is younger, simplify. If the student is older, consider adding more detailed and probing questions.

- Do you feel happy at school?
- Do you have friends?
- Is there anything that you are having trouble with?
- What helps to make you feel happy at school?
- If you could change anything, what would it be?

ASKING THE FAMILY

Another important person to consider interviewing is the parent, caregiver, or guardian. Next to the teacher, they are also the people spending the majority of the time with the child. They may also have insight into what is happening, possible whys, and what has been tried in the past.

There are several things to consider when gathering information from the family. Often, behavior is different at home or in public with the family. This occurs for several reasons. First, home is a completely different setting from school. Home has different expectations, different rules, a different environment, and different people.

Behavior is setting specific. We all engage in what is called code switching,[2] or responding differently to circumstances based on where we are or who we are with. Consider if you use expletives (curse or swear), do you do that at work or with your grandmother around? If you stub your toe, are you a bit more dramatic when someone else is present but can shake off the pain if it is only you?

Behavior is learned, and it is learned predominately through socialization. Who we are with will change how we respond. For example, Sonya's behavior works the same. The hitting is occurring during recess based on that particular environment and not occurring in the classroom because of the specifics of that setting.

Second, home does not have the same demands as school. Few homes have the same amount of structure and work that is required while at school. This will often create different behaviors in those two settings based on the student's ability to handle the demands of school. However, both settings may have times when there is more structure (dinner or going out) and less structure (playing or relaxing). That is information that may help us create our plan.

Parents also have a great deal of insight into what has occurred in the past. What have past teachers done? What works if a parent does see that challenging behavior at home? What does the child say about school? What are his or her likes and dislikes? Is there medical, mental health, or family history information that gives us clues?

Here are some questions to consider when interviewing a parent.

- Have you seen this challenging behavior occur anywhere else but school?
- What strategies do you use to decrease challenging behavior(s)?
- What are the sleeping and eating patterns at home?
- Are there any medical issues that may have an impact at school?
- What does the student say about school at the end of the day?
- What are the student's favorite things to do or people to see?

Additions or modifications to the question can be made based on how the parent is responding and the information that he or she shares. The most important thing is going into the interview with parents free of judgment or bias. Often as the teacher there have been a number of interactions with the family and likely an opinion has been developed regarding their parental responsibilities. Try to remove that bias in order to objectively gather information. Also having a colleague conduct the interview is an option.

Remember that parents may also be struggling every day with the child at home. They too may be exhausted. They too may have additional demands, challenges, fears, and emotions that impact their responses. In most cases, parents and families are doing the best they can with what they know and what they have. Much the way a teacher would not want to be judged on teaching and managing the classroom, the teacher should not judge the family.

The goal is to create a strong partnership with parents and families, become a single voice, and use consistent intervention strategies. Once a successful behavior change process has been developed, the plan can be implemented in other settings, even the home. But the relationship the school staff builds and maintains with the family is vital for that to occur.

The questions that are asked and the people that may have interviewed the student are going to depend on the behavior and the situation. It needs to be determined what is going to be most effective to gather as much information as needed to help see a pattern and find the consistencies. Asking different people who see the student in different places can be beneficial. Asking the student him- or herself can help to strengthen the relationship and find out more personal and emotional information. Garnering information from the family can help to bridge a strong quality of life across school and home.

REFLECTION QUESTIONS

1. What interview questions would you develop for Murray's teacher, Murray, and Murray's parent?
2. What questions would you ask yourself if you were Sonya's teacher?
3. What would you do if a student shared information that you felt could be dangerous or harmful?
4. Create two to three questions to interview the following individuals:

   a. The school administrator (principal)
   b. The specials/electives teacher(s)
   c. The student's friend(s) or classmates

Table 2.2. Completed Settings and Interviews

Setting(s) in which the Target Behavior occurs most often (as described and/or observed by classroom staff)	☒ Classroom ☒ Hallway ☐ Specials/Electives ☒ Playground/Parking Lot ☐ Gym ☐ Cafeteria ☐ Office Areas ☐ Bus/Transportation ☒ Transitions (between activities, between subject areas, between classes, etc.) ☐ Unknown ☐ Other: describe
Anecdotal Report	**Teacher Interview:**
	• How often do you believe, or have you observed, the hitting behavior occurring? *I have seen hitting several times on the playground but I have heard other students mention that they have seen her hit friends. My partner teacher also mentioned one day that she had seen Sonya lash out at a classmate.* • Does hitting only occur during recess or has it been reported or observed in other locations? *I think it happens during times or in places where there is less structure. I see other behaviors in the classroom during transitions and when all the students are together it can be chaotic and overwhelming. It is loud and a bit overstimulating. My partner teacher mentioned that she saw Sonya hit another student in the hallway.*

- What happens right after the hitting? How do adults respond? How do the other students and the victim respond? *In the instances that I have seen the hitting, the student that was hit began crying and yelling, the other students around Sonya got mad at her and told her to stop, and the adult that was monitoring during recess immediately went over and talked to Sonya about how hitting is bad and made her apologize. I don't have much information about the other instances. My partner teacher might be able to share details of what she saw.*
- What strategies have been tried to stop the hitting? *Well, after Sonya has hit, she has had to apologize, she has been removed from the situation, she has lost privileges, and she has gotten a phone call home.*
- How do you feel those have worked? *I'm not sure. The apology made the other student feel better temporarily. But I think that Sonya continues to become more aggressive. While she isn't hitting students in the classroom that I have seen, she has been more confrontational, argumentative, and emotional. I can see her physically lashing out at students in the classroom if something isn't done.*
- Are there other behaviors that you are concerned about? *Hitting is pretty extreme but she also is very disruptive in the class. She wanders around the classroom, she fidgets a lot, and she has a hard time sitting still. And, like I mentioned, she has become more emotional, which can also be disruptive.*
- Where do those most often and least often occur? *Well,· it happens in the classroom but the more I think about it, it starts after we have transitions. When we move from one activity to the next. That is probably most often. Sometimes it happens when the students are doing independent work. She will try to get me to spend more time with her.*

(continued)

Table 2.2.   *Continued*

	• What strategies have been tried to decrease those behaviors? *I feel like I've tried everything. I have moved her seat. I have tried to comfort her. I have used time out, a lot. She has lost privileges. Most often, I think I try to redirect her and get her to refocus. I noticed that when I work with her more one on one, she seems fine.* • What has worked and not worked? *Most of the strategies I described really haven't made it better and I can't work with her one on one all day long. The other students need me too. The only other thing that has worked in the past was going to visit her favorite specials teacher Mrs. Davidson. She loves her! I had her go there one day when she couldn't handle being in my class anymore and she came back after forty-five minutes like a different child.* • Is there any other information that you feel would help to create a plan that you will be implementing? *I just know that I'm exhausted. It is hard trying to focus on Sonya and her needs while also helping everyone else. I need to be able to teach and I most certainly don't want other students to be fearful or scared that they'll be hit or hurt. I've already had two other parents contact me with their concerns.* **Student Interview:** • Do you feel happy at school? *Yah. For the most part. Sometimes I get angry at people because I don't get my way.* • Do you have friends? *Yes. Some days we don't get along but they are my friends still.* • Is there anything that you are having trouble with? *When I get angry I want my teacher to help me and sometimes she doesn't.* • What helps to make you feel happy at school? *My teacher. I like to draw. I wish we could have alpacas in class.* • If you could change anything, what would it be? *Nothing.*

	Parent Interview:
	• Have you seen this challenging behavior occur anywhere else but school? *She is absolutely not allowed to hit in our house. I don't know why this is happening at school but she gets along with her two brothers and has neighborhood friends. I have never seen her be violent toward them. She will have tantrums and get really emotional sometimes if she doesn't get her way but I just figured that was her age.*
	• What strategies do you use to decrease challenging behavior(s)? *If she gets in trouble at home we put her in time out, she has to apologize, she loses her allowance for the week. We also use a chart for her to earn that allowance. She has specific tasks she has to accomplish each week. She likes that because she gets to help me around the house.*
	• What are the sleeping and eating patterns at home? *Okay. There are times that she doesn't sleep well and I know she is cranky and tired but I have to send her to school because I have to work. She eats fine. She is a growing girl.*
	• Are there any medical issues that may have an impact at school? *She goes to the doctor regularly and for things like the cold or flu but she doesn't have any issues. Her father has a temper and they once said that it might be something mental or medical, like ADHD or something.*
	• What does the student say about school at the end of the day? *Most of the time she doesn't say much. Occasionally she has mentioned that she got into a fight with her friends. I never thought that meant hitting.*
	• What are the student's favorite things to do or people to see? *She loves her aunt to death and she likes when we get to go grocery shopping together or go to the store.*

NOTES

1. R. Rosenthal and L. Jacobson, *Pygmalion in the Classroom* (New York: Holt, Rinehart and Winston, 1968); L. Van den Bergh, E. Denessen, L. Hornstra, M. Voeten, and R. W. Holland, "The Implicit Prejudiced Attitudes of Teachers: Relations to Teacher Expectations and the Ethnic Achievement Gap," *American Educational Research Journal* 47, no. 2 (2010): 497–527.

2. A. M. Y. Lin, "Code-Switching in the Classroom: Research Paradigms and Approaches," in *Research Methods in Language and Education, Encyclopedia of Language and Education*, third edition, ed. K. King, Y. J. Lai, and S. May (New York: Springer, 2017).

Chapter Three

The Right Place and the Right Time

Observing the Target Behavior

The child who is not embraced by the village will burn it down to feel its warmth.

—*African proverb*

After defining the behavior and working toward a clearer picture of where and what may be happening through interviews, it is time to observe. Earlier chapters described indirect methods of assessment. This includes asking other people and using memory and judgment of the circumstances surrounding the target behavior. The best way to determine what may be happening and to begin to truly identify the "why" is to directly observe.

There are many benefits to direct observation. First is seeing what is happening in the environment before and after the behavior occurs. Oftentimes, people's memory may be vague or they may not be able to observe all of the fine details that may influence the continuation of the challenging behavior. Sometimes people are too emotionally attached to see the behavior objectively.

Another benefit is the ability to see the behavior across different settings and with different people. A steadfast rule in the observation world is observing the challenging behavior across multiple settings and at different times of the day. Remember the interview questions about the locations and people where the behavior may occur more or less frequently? This is when that information is used to determine where and when observations should be conducted.

Last, patterns can start to be identified through observations. In fact, observation should occur across multiple settings and times of day, thereby with different people until a pattern emerges showing similar things occurring in certain circumstances. These patterns may not always be immediately noticed but most likely there is some repetition as to when and where the challenging behavior occurs. If a pattern is not swiftly evident, either continue to observe or go back to the information already collected and identify whether there are other locations, other people, specific times of day, or even a clearer definition of the behavior that may help to build on the assessment.

The direct observation method is the first step in the data collection process because observing the behavior allows for documentation of what is happening. There are two tools to use when conducting the observations. The first is anecdotal logs, which are notes of the observation. These notes can be rather informal in nature but focus on what is being observed in the environment.

Table 3.1.   Observations

Observation and Data Collection Summary	Observation 1 Date/Time: Setting: Summary of Observation Information: Observation 2 Date/Time: Setting: Summary of Observation Information: Observation 3 Date/Time: Setting: Summary of Observation Information: ABC Data Review/Summary:

OBSERVE AND MEASURE

The conversation so far has not been about the student but rather the behavior. That is because it is important to observe what can be seen and measured. There are many aspects of the student him- or herself that you can't observe. Those are internal states, emotions, feelings, thoughts, and many physiological responses. All of those still occur and they may be very important to why the behavior is occurring. In the world of behavior, however, the goal is to concentrate on what can be seen.

Recall the Dead Man Test or the Potato Test. If a dead man can do it, it isn't behavior. The goal is always to identify the environmental aspects that are observable and measureable. From this list, what is an observable behavior and what is a "potato"?

A. Writing on a worksheet
B. Feeling lonely
C. Pushing a classmate
D. Completing a written assignment
E. Not complying

If you chose A, C, and D, you are correct! Why are B and E not observable behaviors? B is more obvious. A feeling is an internal state that cannot be measured or observed. It can be hypothesized based on the behaviors that may be seen that someone may be feeling lonely. For example, if he or she is sitting alone, crying, attempting to initiate conversation with classmates, or writing a story about being lonely, that internal state of loneliness has a series of observable behaviors that can be seen.

E is a bit more complicated, but it is one of the most common terms used in education: "noncompliance." Noncompliance is seen on office discipline referrals, discussed by teachers, and you've probably even said it yourself. Noncompliance is important, but it isn't a *behavior*.

So what is noncompliance then? How can noncompliance be observed? Again, there are still behaviors that are occurring, but they need to be identified. The student may be verbalizing his or her feelings about not wanting to comply. The student may be engaging in other behaviors than those provided for him or her to do. He or she might be wandering the classroom when he or she should be working on an assignment. He or she might be talking with friends when the teacher is talking. If the focus should be on what can be seen, then someone can still observe what is often referred to as noncompliance.

Another trick to observation is what is called the Hawthorne Effect.[1] This refers to the way in which people change when they are being observed. The reality is, especially for a student that frequently engages in challenging behavior, he or she is likely going to surmise that the person in the room is there to observe him or her. Other students may also react and respond differently to an outsider in the room.

USING THE ABCs

To help adjust to the observation, begin spending short amounts of time with the class. Try not to focus only on the student being observed but rather interact with everyone. As the classroom teacher, be consistent with the responses provided while the data collection process is occurring.

At this time, some anecdotal notes about the behavior can be taken. Have paper and pencil ready or use an electronic device such as a mobile phone or tablet. There are many apps now for mobile phones and tablets that can help with collecting anecdotal information.

For the first few minutes or even times that an observation occurs, write as much as can be seen. Focus on the entire classroom. It is important to document some of the influencing factors in the classroom that may impact why the behavior is occurring. These factors may include areas like the layout of the classroom, the noise level, how transitions occur, and the pace of instruction. This information can be added to the notes prior to the start of the observation so that the data can be used later to better understand the triggers for the challenging behavior.

After spending some time just noticing, documenting, and note taking, the observation can include more organization with the ABC data collection method.[2] Without too much technical talk, the A stands for Antecedent. An antecedent is what happens in the environment right before the target behavior happens. The B stands for Behavior. This will be the *one* target behavior that you are focused on—the behavior that has already been identified and defined. The C stands for Consequence.

Unlike in the education field, in the behavior world, consequence does not have a negative connotation. It is not a consequence that happens because someone was naughty. Consequence is what happens right after the behavior.

A: Antecedent (before)
B: Behavior (target/challenging)
C: Consequence (after)

The best way to collect ABC data is to use a three-column chart. There are many premade charts on the internet and, again, there are apps that can be used with mobile devices. A simple way is to use a piece of paper and create three columns. Put an A above one column, a B above the middle column, and a C above the last column. In the B column, write the behavior that is being focused on for observation. It will look something like table 3.2 but likely end up with many more rows.

Table 3.2.   Blank ABC Chart

A: Antecedent	B: Behavior	C: Consequence
	Hitting	
	Hitting	
	Hitting	
	Hitting	

Use the first and third columns to organize the observation. Concentrate on what is being observed immediately before and immediately after the behavior. Again, the data should be collected in multiple settings and at different times. Use a different chart for each location. This will ensure that the observer can begin to see any patterns. Do the same antecedents trigger the hitting behavior? Does the same thing happen after the behavior? Do different people have different responses?

Table 3.3. Completed ABC Chart

A: Antecedent	B: Behavior	C: Consequence
Classmate approaches Sonya with a ball	Hitting	Student cries Adult reprimands
Classmate cuts in front of Sonya in line	Hitting	Student yells Adult reprimands
Sonya runs to desk and bumps into classmate	Hitting	Student pushes back
Classmate approaches Sonya with a toy	Hitting	Adult reprimands

There may not be many data points in this example, but patterns can already begin to emerge. Most often when Sonya is approached or in close proximity with a classmate, there is hitting behavior, which is most often followed by a reaction from a peer and a reprimand from the teacher. Remember that the exact same thing will not happen every time; instead look for enough of a pattern of As and Cs to determine that the data accurately represent what most often occurs before and after the challenging behavior in different settings and at different times.

Both the anecdotal and ABC direct observation data will build onto the understanding of why this challenging behavior may be occurring. Each step in the assessment process gets closer to identifying the "why," but first it is necessary to fully understand the "what." What is occurring? Observations will assist in becoming familiar with the patterns and environment.

REFLECTION QUESTIONS

1. Create an ABC data collection chart and complete a sample for Murray's behavior.
2. What would you do if you were unable to observe the challenging behavior in the locations and times that you have been available to observe?
3. What would you do if a clear pattern is not emerging from your observations?
4. What are some ways that you feel could help to avoid the Hawthorne Effect?

Table 3.4. Completed Observations

Observation and Data Collection Summary	Observation 1 Date/Time: 11/16 Setting: Transition from Class to Outside Summary of Observation Information: *Sonya was the line leader. A number of students complained. The teacher and adult volunteer in the classroom did not notice the disturbance until Sonya had pushed a student. The process to line up was a bit chaotic. There was also a fire alarm during the morning prior to this observation.* Observation 2 Date/Time: 12/1 Setting: Classroom Summary of Observation Information: *Sonya appeared to be sleeping when the observation began. The class was instructed to build a model of a building out of popsicle sticks. Sonya was talking loudly with classmates. Classmates did not appear to engage with Sonya. Sonya spent approximately five minutes wandering around the classroom. The teacher pulled Sonya aside and spoke with her about getting along with classmates.* Observation 3 Date/Time: 12/3 Setting: Outside Summary of Observation Information: *Sonya was playing on the outside equipment. Classmates were not interacting with her. Sonya appeared to become angry or frustrated. She clenched her fists, her face became red, and she began to vocalize loudly. One classmate told the adult nearby and that adult went and spoke with Sonya about how to play with others.* ABC Data Review/Summary: *Most often when Sonya is approached or in close proximity with a classmate there is hitting behavior, which is most often followed by a reaction from a peer and a reprimand from the teacher.*

NOTES

1. J. McCambridge, J. Witton, and D. R. Elbourne, "Systematic Review of the Hawthorne Effect: New Concepts Are Needed to Study Research Participation Effects," *Journal of Clinical Epidemiology* 67, no. 3 (2014): 267–77.

2. L. K. Chandler and C. M. Dahlquist, *Functional Assessment: Strategies to Prevent and Remediate Challenging Behavior in School Settings*, second edition (Upper Saddle River, NJ: Merrill Prentice Hall, 2006).

Chapter Four

At a Glance

Visualizing the Data

Our job is not to toughen our children up to face a cruel and heartless world. Our job is to raise children who will make the world a little less cruel and heartless.

—*L. R. Knost*

Human behavior is complex. There are often multiple challenging behaviors that may be competing or coexisting. In the assessment process it is important to prioritize a target behavior. This doesn't mean that all other behaviors will be ignored or won't be addressed; it means that the MDT or teacher should work to identify the most significant challenging behavior.

There are two ways to classify and think about how to determine the most significant challenging behavior. The first is: What is the behavior that occurs the most frequently? The second is: What is the behavior that has the greatest impact on the classroom? This process was begun in chapter 1 with defining the behavior.

Table 4.1.   Data Collection

Data Collection Tools	Description of Data Collection Method

• ABC Data
• Can't Do vs. Won't Do
• Event Recording, Frequency
  ◦ Exact
  ◦ Whole Interval
  ◦ Partial Interval
• Duration
• Latency
• Intensity
	Used (baseline data should be graphed and inserted in this area):

There are a number of reasons why visualization of data is an essential part of the assessment process. The first is to be able to focus on one behavior. There are already enough demands for teachers in the classroom to manage and student needs to address. It would not be efficient or realistic to have to monitor multiple behavior assessments and plans for one student.

Second, if the most significant challenging behavior can be addressed, decreased, and then maintained with an effective plan, then the next behavior may be addressed. Last, choosing to address the most significant behavior (the one that occurs the most or has the greatest impact) has the ability to improve the student's quality of life. Quality of life for the student, the other students in the classroom, and the teacher is one of the driving forces of developing sound behavior assessments and intervention plans.

The best tool to drive this work is data. Data may seem scary at first. Collecting data may feel like an unnecessary step. Data are the backbone of the assessment process or could be considered the brain of the process. The brain helps to connect all the body's working systems. Data perform a similar function. The data are what are collected from the environment, like the signals that trigger in the brain. Then data are used to help make decisions, like the signals that trigger the body to move, sleep, laugh, or cry.

A side note and important point: The word data is already in its plural form. The singular for data is datum, and no one says datum! When using the plural form of data, be sure to attach the correct tense. *Data are. Data were.* It may seem nitpicky, but it will make you sound really impressive when you are chatting with all of your data geek friends at the weekend data parties!

In fact, the ABC data collection process that was shared in chapter 3 was the beginning of sending these signals to the brain. ABC data can continue to be collected if they are helpful for making decisions. However, they can be a bit cumbersome to maintain in a busy classroom. It can be laborious to write down so much detail. ABC data are best to help better understand what happens before and after the target behavior. Once there is a clear pattern in those data, other data tools can be used to ease the process.

Choosing a data collection tool can seem overwhelming. There are so many data files stored in the brain, how does one know which to choose for the target behavior? To begin, it is necessary to know the different types of data collection tools available.

CAN'T DO VERSUS WON'T DO

One tool that can be used is often described as the can't do, won't do[1] assessment. It is not a formalized data collection tool, but much like ABC data, it can be used to help make decisions about next steps once the intervention planning has begun. It can also help to understand if it is a skill versus a willingness to perform the skill; it helps to determine if there is a need to remediate skills or teach new skills.

A simple way to collect information about skill and will is to set up a type of experiment. One effective way is to provide challenging work to the student and let him or her know that if he or she completes a portion of it, he or she will earn a favorite reward. The reward will need to be something the student would really want to work for.

If, even with a powerful reward, the student is unable to perform the task, there is likely a skill issue. If the student completes the task and earns the reward, the student would be considered to have a will issue. Another way to gather this information is to ask other professionals that work with the student. Do they believe that it is a skill deficit or a motivation deficit? If, even with a powerful reward the student is still unable to perform the task, there is likely a skill issue.

Think about it like this—if offered ten million dollars right now, could you engineer a working spaceship? If the answer is no, there is probably a lack of the skills necessary, so teaching the new skills to appropriately complete the task would be important. If the answer is yes, for that amount of money anything can be created, then it is likely that ten million dollars is a strong enough motivator to make even challenging work worth it.

The can't do versus won't do is not traditional data collection, but it can be used as a key decision-making tool. That is truly what data are. They are the tools—those signals to the brain that inform us about our next steps, which decisions to make, which direction to go. ABC and can't/won't are informal data tools, but even the more formal data collection tools don't have to be intimidating.

EVENT RECORDING, FREQUENCY

Think of event recording as the first stop in data collection, the most commonly used tool in the toolbox, and one of the easiest tools to use. Event recording is a fancy way of saying tally marking. Event recording is as simple as making a check or tally or checking a box each time the challenging behavior occurs. Frequency adds the element of time. Frequency is event recording within a certain time frame, for example, from 9:00 a.m. to 10:00 a.m. or only during science.

Frequency is then the number of behaviors within that time period divided by the length of time.

$$\frac{38 \text{ instances of calling out}}{2 \text{ hours } (120 \text{ minutes})} = 31.66 \text{ or } 32\% \text{ of the time}$$

The best time to use event recording or frequency is when the behavior has a clear beginning and clear end. In other words, it is easy to count.

Remember Sonya? *"Sonya is <u>constantly interrupting</u> instruction. She bounces in her seat <u>all day long</u>, if she can even <u>stay in it</u>. She's even been hitting <u>another child</u> during recess lately. I can't get any teaching done with her in the classroom."* There are some good data cues to use in the description of her behavior. For example, words like "constantly" and "all day" as well as information about the behavior, like "hitting." These help us to determine if we want to count how many.

There are also different types of event recording. Exact count means that you count every single instance of the behavior. This can be difficult to do in a busy classroom while instruction is going on. Partial and whole interval allow for observation of the behavior within certain intervals of time. This is really helpful when the behavior occurs a lot. Partial interval is a record of whether the behavior occurred or did not occur at any time during the intervals.

Because Sonya's behavior is labeled as "constant," partial interval[2] may be helpful. Break a time period into intervals. An hour is chunked into five-minute intervals (that is, twelve time periods per hour). Have a timer handy to track each five-minute interval. If the behavior occurred *at all* during a five-minute interval, mark that box.

Whole interval[3] uses the same time chunking process, but the behavior is only marked if it is observed during *the entire* interval of time. If an hour is chunked into five-minute intervals, the box would only be marked if the behavior occurs within the five minutes and lasts for *the entire* five minutes.

Table 4.2.   Whole Interval Recording

Student Name: Observation Date: Target Behavior:								
9:00–9:05	+	–	9:21–9:25	+	–	9:41–9:45	+	–
9:06–9:10	+	–	9:26–9:30	+	–	9:46–9:50	+	–
9:11–9:15	+	–	9:31–9:35	+	–	9:51–9:55	+	–
9:16–9:20	+	–	9:36–9:40	+	–	9:56–10:00	+	–

DURATION

Duration is another helpful data tool. This is a measurement of how long a behavior may occur. Duration or length of the behavior is best for behaviors that last over time. The description of Sonya's behavior of "constantly" interrupting and bouncing "all day long" may be good indicators that duration could be used to measure the behavior.

For example, it may be helpful in Sonya's case to start a timer the first time the challenging behavior is noticed and then stop the timer once the behavior has ceased. While it may be hard at first to pay attention to when to start and stop the timer, having a good understanding of the definition of the challenging behavior and knowing when it is most and least likely to occur will help to create the most efficient way to collect duration data.

LATENCY

Latency of behavior is best used to determine the length of time between a cue or direction and the start of the behavior. For instance, how long is it before a student begins working on a task after the teacher provides the instruction? Latency can also be used to better understand the delay between prompt and action. If Murray was asked to begin his bell work because he had been spending too much time joking with his friends, latency would be the time between the teacher asking Murray to begin and when Murray begins the task.

INTENSITY

Intensity is a measure of how much of a behavior. It may be necessary to measure the intensity of the sound or decibel of noise. It may be necessary to measure the magnitude of the behavior. For example, Sonya is bouncing in her seat. Is the magnitude minor? Is Sonya just fidgeting at her seat or is the magnitude major; is she shaking the walls? Intensity is often measured in sequential levels to better understand the behavior like, low, medium, and high or mild, moderate, and severe.

SCATTERPLOT

A great tool to use to capture a mix of important data is called a scatterplot. Scatterplots will show both frequency and duration along with when the behavior occurs. Often a scatterplot is preferred in a classroom setting because it both collects data and shows a visual representation of those data.

Table 4.3. Scatterplot

Student Name: _____
Classroom: _____
Date: _____

Subject	Time	Calling Out	Calling Out	Calling Out	Calling Out	Calling Out
Math	9–10	X				
Art	10–11	X	X	X	X	
Reading	11–12		X			X
Writing	1–2	X				

Calling out did not occur ☐
Calling out occurred one time ☒

The scatterplot in table 4.3 allows for the behavior to be seen across time. Additional components can be added like coloring in the box if the behavior occurs more than one time or using a half of an "x" or a slash mark if the behavior occurs for the full time. The scatterplot tool can be customized to help track more complex behaviors or develop a better understanding of the behavior over time.

It is also important to note that a combination of data collection methods should be used to best understand the behavior (for example, collecting both frequency and duration of a single behavior). In the case of Sonya, data collection involves collecting how often she is observed bouncing in her chair by tallying on a piece of paper or indicating how long the bouncing lasts. This can be done by adding a start and stop time next to the tally when you are able to observe the duration; the intensity of the challenging behavior could also be included by writing the magnitude of the behavior.

On one small piece of paper, even a napkin if all else fails, you could collect the frequency, duration, and intensity of a single behavior. If you were to collect those data over several days, you would likely see a clear pattern of how much, how long, and how intense the behavior typically is.

Other tools that can assist in making data collection easier can be either high tech or low tech. The example in table 4.3 is a rather low-tech tool; all you need is something to write on and something to write with. There are also some higher-tech tools that can come in handy when tracking behavior. Things like mobile applications and websites can assist with data collection. Other low- and high-tech tools to help with data collection include what is shown in table 4.4.

Table 4.4. Data Collection Tools

Frequency	• golf or people counter • pennies or paper clips moved from one pocket to another • calculator • adding beans or beads to a jar • data application for mobile devices
Duration and Latency	• watch or stopwatch • timer
Intensity	• decibel meter • website noise meter

Once the right tool has been chosen, there are some data collection rules of thumb to follow. In chapter 2, there were some initial observations to capture information about how to define the behavior. Those data can now be used to help determine when and how to collect the baseline data.

Baseline data are those data that allow us to see what is happening before any interventions or changes are made. It is like weighing yourself for several weeks before you start a new diet. You want to capture what is happening now so you can compare it to after the change.

A general rule for data collection is to capture enough data to see a clear pattern. Many times people ask, *"how long do I need to collect data?"* Well, that is a very tough question. Sometimes behavior occurs very frequently or rapidly, so it is easy to draw hypotheses from small sets of data. However, sometimes behaviors occur rarely, though they are severe, so it can take days, weeks, or even months to see a clear pattern.

Consider if Murray from earlier chapters has a challenged home life. Perhaps his parents had to relinquish their rights to aged grandparents. Maybe Murray gets to see his birth parents every once in a while and when he does he has to travel a great distance and doesn't feel like he has a strong bond or close relationship with them so he struggles each visit.

While he has challenging behavior (mouthing off) that occurs frequently, he also has some more severe behavior that occurs once a month or so. If using frequency data to collect the verbalization behavior, there would likely be enough data to understand the pattern after a brief period of time. If additional data were not collected over time, then it could be that the pattern of the challenging behavior that occurs approximately once a month would cause data and problem solving to be lost.

What is a "clear pattern"? A clear pattern means that the data are trending in the same direction consistently. Another rule of thumb is that there should be *at least* three data points to begin to see a behavioral pattern. In these three examples (figures 4.1, 4.2, and 4.3), it is demonstrated why it is necessary to identify patterns.

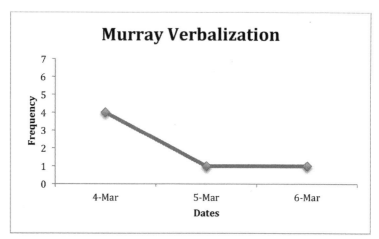

Figure 4.1. Graphed Data

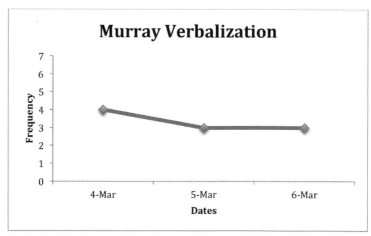

Figure 4.2. Graphed Data

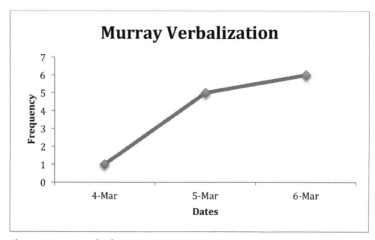

Figure 4.3. Graphed Data

In figure 4.1 you can see that the third data point is going down, or what would be called a downward trend. Figure 4.2 shows steady data, not too much upward or too much downward. Figure 4.3 shows the last data point going upward.

In this case, we are looking at the target or challenging behavior of Murray's vocalizations. This is also considered baseline data, or data that are collected prior to any intervention or change. Baseline data help to better understand what is currently happening so that as the process progresses there are clear pictures of the change following the intervention. Data will be collected throughout the FBA and the BIP so that the MDT can consistently be making data-based decisions.

If we were collecting baseline data, these three data points may not be enough to show us a clear trend, so more data would be collected. In all three graphs there are some assumptions that could be made but more data would help to clarify. For instance, in figure 4.1 the target behavior appears to be "getting better," so there wouldn't be much need to intervene. In figure 4.3, the target behavior appears to be getting worse, so an intervention may be necessary. But there are only three data points.

Figure 4.4 shows the same data from figure 4.2 but with the additional days of data collection. A different pattern emerged with more data collected. If more data hadn't been collected, an MDT could have spent time, money, and energy on an intervention that was not based on accurate information. This happens all too often. While data collection may take time, it is vital to the process.

The graph utilized is just as important as the data graphed. Why? The goal of graphing data is to be able to make data-based decisions. Remember that

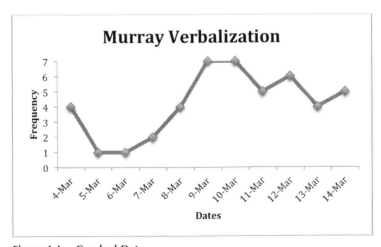

Figure 4.4.   Graphed Data

these data-based decisions are also being made as a team. Everyone on the MDT should be able to clearly identify trends and patterns from the data.

While most people are probably more comfortable or familiar with a pie chart or a bar graph, the line graph is the common tool used to analyze behavioral data. Line graphs allow you to see multiple data sets, trends, and subtle changes in the data.

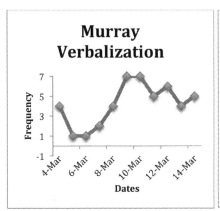
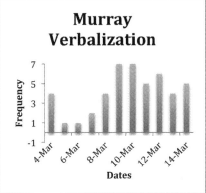

Figure 4.5.   Graphed Data Comparison

Figure 4.5 shows the same set of data represented in two different graphs. While you can still see the change in frequency on both graphs, the trend is much more visible in the line graph. There may also be times when graphing multiple sets of data are needed and the line graph allows for the connections to be seen.

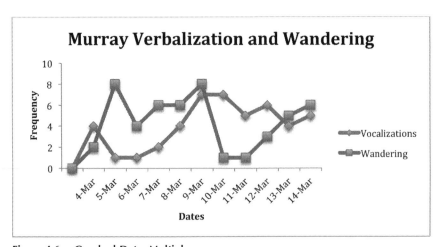

Figure 4.6.   Graphed Data, Multiple

From these data in figure 4.6, it becomes clear that verbalizations (or excessive talking and noise) and wandering in the classroom may be impacting each other. For instance, there are several days when the behaviors occurred at nearly the same rate. Some hypotheses may begin to be drawn from these data.

The MDT should also strive for easy visualizations so that when a student's parents, caregivers, or loved ones become involved in meetings and decision making, it is clear to them why decisions are being made. Building a strong parent partnership is crucial and can be an important step in the FBA/BIP process. This is especially true if the FBA/BIP process includes wrap-around supports. If the data are clear, easy to understand, and transparent, it may help to build trust and confidence for the entire MDT in the FBA/BIP process.

Data collection and data graphing can be easy or complicated. Work smarter, not harder. Begin with the easiest data collection tool and then work up, adding in more data collection tools and processes as needed. There are also a number of websites and resources online that can help in finding the right data tool, making the right data decisions, and utilizing spreadsheets to create graphs. Graphing data can eventually encompass multiple data sets, intervention change lines, trend lines, and so much more. But all of that is not necessary, at least not yet.

REFLECTION QUESTIONS

1. Based on what you have learned about Sonya's behavior, determine the data collection tool that you would use, create a set of data, and graph it.
2. Find an example of a blank scatterplot online and spend the day tracking a friend or family member's behavior (for example, cell phone use, asking a question, nail biting, etc.).
3. If you notice that a student in your class took excessive breaks (using the restroom, using a hall pass, etc.), what behavior collection tool would you use and why?
4. You are preparing for a meeting with Murray's father and aunt. Murray's behavior has been getting worse over the past couple of weeks. You have the graphed data ready to present. Write down the important points that you want to discuss about the data. What are the patterns and trends that you notice? What about the timing or days of the week? How will you explain why you have spent time collecting data rather than intervening?

Data Collection Method and Graphs	Description of Data Collection Method Used (Baseline data should be graphed and inserted in this area):

Data Collection Tools
• ABC Data
• Can't Do v. Won't Do
• Event Recording, Frequency
   o Exact
   o Whole Interval
   o Partial Interval
• Duration
• Latency
• Intensity
	Data included frequency, ABC data
	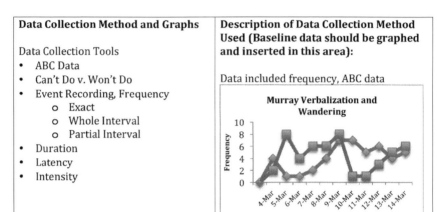

Figure 4.7.   Completed Data Collection

NOTES

1. A. M. VanDerHeyden and J. C. Witt, "Best Practices in Can't Do/Won't Do Assessment," in *Best Practices in School Psychology*, fifth edition, ed. A. Thomas and J. Grimes (Bethesda, MD: National Association of School Psychologists, 2008), 131–40.

2. John O. Cooper, Timothy E. Heron, and William L. Heward, *Applied Behavior Analysis* (Upper Saddle River, NJ: Pearson/Merrill-Prentice Hall, 2007).

3. Cooper, Heron, and Heward, *Applied Behavior Analysis*.

Chapter Five

Hypothesizing the "Why" and Determining the Function

The children who need the most love will ask for it in the most unloving ways.

—*Russel Barkley*

Now that you have defined the behavior, determined where and when it is occurring, and collected and analyzed baseline data, it is time to figure out what it all means. In the functional *assessment* process there is no definitive answer but rather an educated guess based on data. The steps that have been taken so far will lead to a hypothesis about the potential function of behavior. The data will help to draw the best hypothesis.

Table 5.1.   Hypothesis Statement

Function of Behavior (as determined by data, record review, interviews, hypothesis statement)	Attention (Adults) ☐
	Attention (Peers) ☐
Tools to assist with function determination: • Competing Behaviors Pathway • FAST • MAS • QABF	Escape/Avoid ☐
	Tangible ☐
	Sensory ☐
Hypothesis Statement or Target Behavior	When (setting/environmental factors) _____ the student will (target behavior) _____ in order to gain (function) _____ as supported by (data utilized) _____.

In your mind, or even out loud, you have probably already tried to attach a function to the behavior of Murray and Sonya. You may feel as though you have had a Sonya or a Murray in your class and it is obvious that they just want *this* or *that*. All too often in the FBA process, people jump to the hypothesis phase before truly taking the time to understand the "what." Did you notice that there are four chapters leading up to this one?

With so many TV dramas designed to capture your inner sleuth to be the solver of the mystery, it is easy to want to jump ahead throughout the process and solve the problem. When conclusions are drawn too early, however, resources can be spent and used ineffectively. If Detective So-and-So drew his hypothesis after finding the first clue, he'd likely be wrong, and it would make for a pretty quick and boring TV show.

This is the time to pull together all the information that has been collected and put the pieces of the puzzle in one place. And if you have been secretly telling yourself that you know the "why," now is the time to see if you and the data match. Thankfully, there are additional tools that can assist in determining the hypothesized function of behavior.

Think of this process like creating a painting. There are layers of color and imagery that are necessary to fully capture the setting sun or the blooming flowers on the mountainside. Each brushstroke is part of a larger image that is only unveiled and recognizable at the end. Each brushstroke is placed on the canvas in an order that develops the foundational colors, the lowlights and highlights, the thickness of the paint. The functional assessment components are those foundational layers.

The initial strokes of paint on the canvas were to help define the challenging (target) behavior, ensuring that the behavior is described in a way that is observable and measurable. This definition of the target behavior is the foundation, the start of the process that will be built on.

Next, time was spent exploring where the behavior occurs and asking people familiar with the student to help develop a better understanding. Through this process, information about the setting event is typically discovered. The setting events are things that happen before the antecedents that may trigger or worsen the challenging behavior.

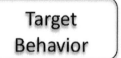

Figure 5.1.   Target Behavior

There can be both slow and fast triggers. Common triggers include lack of sleep, hunger, illness, medications, specific subjects in school, etc. The settings events "set the stage" for the challenging behavior. In the case of Sonya, being present on the playground appeared to be a setting event. Understanding the setting event is important, but it may not be something that there is much control over. For Murray, the visitation with his family was a possible trigger for challenging behaviors. A teacher can't ask a parent to stop or start a medication or monitor a child's sleeping patterns; it is helpful to know, but ultimately the antecedent is the driver.

Figure 5.2.   Setting Event

In chapter 3, observing the behavior and determining what was happening before and after were introduced. The antecedent is the "thing" that occurs immediately before the behavior. It "cues" the behavior. The antecedent is the bell on the microwave that cues you to open the door and get your tea or dinner. The antecedent is the raised hand that cues the classroom to look up and listen. The antecedent is the timer that reminds a student that recess is over and it is time to line up or that this period is done and it is time to walk to the next class.

Figure 5.3.   Antecedent

The next layer on the canvas is the consequence. The consequence is what happens directly after the behavior. It is neutral, meaning it is not tied to a "good thing" or a "bad thing." It is simply what occurs directly after the target behavior.

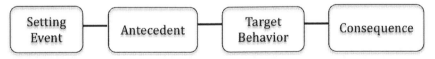

Figure 5.4.   Consequence

This is the beginning of what is often referred to as a competing pathway of behavior.[1] Later, additional pieces will be included to help build out more layers of support. For now, this is the foundation for your assessment, the foundation to understanding "why" the challenging behavior is occurring. Remember that the function of behavior is the "why." The function is the consequence and is what maintains the behavior. It is the payoff. In the ABCs of behavior, the function is the C.

There are most commonly four functions of behavior. Some researchers[2] and practitioners have included additional categories, but the seminal works of behavior analysis have stuck with four.

Table 5.2.   Functions of Behavior

Attention (peers and/or adults)	Behaving in a way that will garner or focus the attention of others onto the individual.
Avoidance/Escape	Avoid: Behaving in a way that avoids an activity or person *prior to* the presence of the person or activity. Escape: Behaving in a way that allows a person to *leave the presence* of a person or activity.
Tangible	Behaving in a way that produces access to a tangible item or activity.
Sensory	Behaving in a way that produces access or removal of a sensory stimulation (sound, light, touch, feel, etc.).

Human behavior is complex. There are often multiple functions working collaboratively to create a cluster of behaviors and consequences. It can get muddy and easy to overcomplicate and overthink. Remember that simpler is almost always better. Also remember that this is only a hypothesis. Unless a full functional analysis is staged and completed, it is the data that are guiding the hypothesis development.

In the process of hypothesizing the function of the behavior or the "why," it will be necessary to determine what is the *most likely* function maintaining the behavior. In reviewing the data, determine which consequence occurs most often. In fleshing out the function, for example, be specific if the attention is most often coming from the student's peers or from the adults. Determine whether the student avoids (before) or escapes (during) a nonpreferred activity.

Sensory is often the most complicated function, as it can be hard to see—pun intended! When considering if something sensory is maintaining the challenging behavior, ask this question: "If no one else was in the room, if there was nothing in the room, would the student still try to gain access to something sensory?" In other words, in absence of anything else, would the student still hum to gain access to noise or pinch his or her skin to gain access to touch/feeling?

How does one go about determining the function? Data! Review the data that have been collected and they will provide hints. In the C column of the ABC chart, does it refer a lot to "teacher reprimands" or "teacher speaks with"? That is likely adult attention. Does the C column say things like "student removed from class" or "student left room/area"? That is likely avoidance or escape.

There are also some additional tools that can help. There are three commonly used assessments that partnered with the data can paint a pretty complete picture of the function. The three most common assessments are: the Motivation Assessment Scale (MAS),[3] the Functional Assessment Screening Tool (FAST),[4] and the Questions About Behavioral Function (QABF).[5] They can all be found online and are quick and easy to use.

Each of the tools asks a series of questions to better understand what may be maintaining the behavior. They require asking questions about the behavior with the teacher and sometimes family or others that know the student well. They are also best used in combination; although many people have preferences as to which they use most often, it is recommended to use at least two to corroborate the hypothesized function.

With the data that have been collected and the extra tools used to determine the function, the picture should be fairly clear and a hypothesis statement can be created. The hypothesis statement should follow a clear pattern. It should include the information about the setting and any environmental factors that may impact the behavior. It should include the target behavior and hypothesized function. And it should include how those conclusions were drawn and what are the data that support the hypothesis. For example, use this sentence structure:

When (setting/environmental factors), the student will (target behavior) in order to gain (function) as supported by (data utilized).

When Sonya is on the playground or in unstructured settings with few adults, she will hit other students in order to gain attention from her peers as supported by ABC, baseline, and MAS/FAST data.

When Murray is in the classroom during instructional time and after he has visited his parents, he will make loud and disruptive vocalizations in order to escape a nonpreferred task as supported by ABC, baseline, and QABF data.

Once the MDT have established the hypothesis statement and determined the hypothesized function of the behavior, it is time to begin planning interventions and supports. The assessment is the foundation, the beginning colors on the canvas, but the behavior intervention plan are the details that make the painting come to life.

REFLECTION QUESTIONS

1. Search online to find the assessment tools described in this chapter (MAS, FAST, QABF). Which do you prefer? Why?

2. Describe how you would know if the attention is maintained more by adults or more by peers. What are clues you would look for? Why?
3. How would you know if the function of a challenging behavior such as self-injury was sensory?

Table 5.3. Completed Function of Behavior

Function of Behavior (as determined by data, record review, interviews, hypothesis statement) Tools to assist with function determination: • Competing Behaviors Pathway • FAST • MAS • QABF	Attention (Adults) ☐ Attention (Peers) ☒ Escape/Avoid ☐ Tangible ☐ Sensory ☐
Hypothesis Statement or Target Behavior	When Sonya is on the playground or in unstructured settings with few adults, she will hit other students in order to gain attention from her peers as supported by ABC, baseline, and MAS/FAST data.

NOTES

1. https://www.pbis.org/resource/1091/competing-behavior-pathway-and-behavior-support-plan.
2. J. Cooper, T. Heron, and W. Heward, *Applied Behavior Analysis* (Hoboken, NJ: Pearson Education, 2007); R. O'Neill, R. Horner, R. Albin, J. Sprague, K. Storey, and J. Newton, *Functional Assessment and Program Development for Problem Behavior: A Practical Handbook* (Pacific Grove, CA: Brooks/Cole Publishing Company, 1997).
3. r4analyzingbehavior.wikispaces.com/file/view/MAS.pdf.
4. www.cmhcm.org/userfiles/filemanager/961/.
5. https://www.liberty.k12.ga.us/ourpages/auto/2016/2/1/43422828/Doc_%20 5%20QABF%20Questions%20About%20Behavioral%20Functions.pdf.

Part II

BEHAVIOR INTERVENTION PLAN

Chapter Six

Planning the How

Developing a BIP

All behaviors are logical in the larger context, and it's our job to help kids find more productive behaviors. Kids are not their behaviors.

—*Ellen Berg, Educator*

With all of the data gathered and analyzed, a hypothesis statement and understanding of the function of behavior developed, it is now time to begin to cultivate the behavior intervention plan (BIP). A BIP is more than just a collection of ideas to address the challenging behavior. The BIP should be a step-by-step guide of what to do (and not do) when the challenging behavior occurs. It should be mapped, planned, and written in a way that anyone could implement the plan. It should include enough detail to be clear on what to do but not include so many details that it is overwhelming to the people implementing the plan. It should clarify what to do in the best case scenario, when the appropriate behavior is being displayed, and in the worst case scenario, when the challenging behavior or crisis behavior is displayed.

The painting was developed through the functional assessment. That process allowed you to see a clear picture of what is happening. The behavior plan is the roadmap. It is the process to know what to do and when.

The behavior plan *must* align to the assessment findings. Although they are two separate components of the process, the two must share information. If the behavior was easily hypothesized and did not require the full assessment, the behavior plan must still connect back to the hypothesized function. One of the ways to assist in making those connections is to recap and build from the FBA.

Table 6.1.   Highlights of FBA

Sources of Information: (List sources of information used in FBA, both formal and informal, to develop this plan)
Strength Based Profile: (Identify skills and interests, positive relationships, prosocial behaviors, family and community supports, and other protective factors)
Functional Behavioral Assessment (FBA) Summary Statement: (Describe specific problem behavior and summary/hypothesis statement from FBA)

The sources of data and information that were used on the functional assessment can be both the formal observations and data collected and the informal anecdotal information. While direct observation is the best indicator for understanding behavior, the information collected from informal interviews and the survey information gathered from the teacher are also relevant and important.

Teachers often spend more time with a child than the family given the hours of compulsory education. Given that depth of time and wealth of interaction, teachers' "intuition" can be a valuable addition to the development of a plan. Oftentimes teachers may know nuances or minute triggers that others may not observe. Teachers are able to see the daily interactions, social circles, fluctuations of power, and interplay of characteristics on a daily—if not minute-to-minute—basis. This heightens the understanding of what may work and may not work when developing a plan.

Teachers also know the strengths and skills of the student. Every plan should begin with the student in mind. While a teacher may be frustrated and upset because a child has been exhibiting challenging behavior—behavior that may be rude, distasteful, hurtful, or even aggressive—he or she is still a human being with strengths, skills, abilities, beauty, and hope. He or she is still a child.

Consider that developmentally children are often seeking two things: knowledge and boundaries. Childhood is built on the ability to learn new things and push limits. Childhood also continues well into the development of early adulthood. The teenage, adolescent, and young adult brain is like a chocolate cake in the oven; it may on the outside *appear* to be cooked all the way through, but when you stick the toothpick in the middle, there is still a bit of mushy center that needs to keep developing.

From daycare, preschool, and prekindergarten all the way to (and maybe even through) college, students need a balance of guidance and limits. Students will push past that guidance and beyond those limits, so our plans should account for their unique and individualized needs.

The plan should be developed to meet students where they are and take them to where they need to go. In other words, the behavior intervention plan should be

- individualized,
- based on current and accurate data,
- aligned to the function of behavior, and
- clear and concise.

One of the strategies to individualize a plan and ensure that the team is focused on student strengths is to develop and write it to pass the birthday test. The birthday test means that the description of the student's strengths, skills, likes, and dislikes is clear enough that any person reading it would know what to buy the student for his or her birthday.

It may seem silly or difficult, but if the team is truly focused on improving the quality of life for the student and ensuring that he or she is engaging in socially and developmentally appropriate behavior, the plan should reflect a depth of knowledge and care about the student that is clear. It should pass the birthday test. Here is an example for Sonya.

Sonya is full of life and energy. She has a strong desire to learn and interact with her peers. She loves her family and speaks of them often. She enjoys drawing, coloring, and crafting and often incorporates her two dogs into her art. Sonya thrives in a classroom that is structured and rulebound. She forms immediate bonds with adults. Sonya is able to participate in all classroom activities. Sonya enjoys leadership roles and being "the princess."

From this description, what would you buy Sonya for her birthday? What information could help you to develop an intervention plan? Let's look at Murray.

Murray has strong connections to his peers. He believes strongly in loyalty and friendship. He has strong will toward independence and prefers to learn through experience. Murray is creative and energetic. He performs magic and is a skilled skateboarder. Murray has developed strong bonds to specific family members and will incorporate childhood memories into his writing. He is imaginative and a big picture thinker. Murray prefers opportunities to work with partners and have collaborative projects.

From this description, do you know what you would bring to Murray's birthday party? Were there clues about how to build an intervention plan for him? Was everything framed positively?

Table 6.2. Strengths and Skills

Description of the **Challenging Behavior**	Description of the **Student**
Sonya is constantly interrupting instruction. She bounces in her seat all day long, if she can even stay in it. She's even been hitting another child during recess lately. I can't get any teaching done with her in the classroom.	Sonya is full of life and energy. She has a strong desire to learn and interact with her peers. She loves her family and speaks of them often. She enjoys drawing, coloring, and crafting and often incorporates her two dogs into her art. Sonya thrives in a classroom that is structured and rulebound. She forms immediate bonds with adults. Sonya is able to participate in all classroom activities. Sonya enjoys leadership roles and being "the princess."
Murray is always mouthing off in class. He thinks he's the class clown. Every time I am instructing he has something smart to say. I can't keep him in my class if he's always going to be disrespectful.	Murray has strong connections to his peers. He believes strongly in loyalty and friendship. He has strong will toward independence and prefers to learn through experience. Murray is creative and energetic. He performs magic and is a skilled skateboarder. Murray has developed strong bonds to specific family members and will incorporate childhood memories into his writing. He is imaginative and a big picture thinker. Murray prefers opportunities to work with partners and have collaborative projects.

THE BRAIN AND BEHAVIOR

The first thing to notice in table 6.2 is the difference in length of the descriptions. Of course the information about the student and the student's strengths and skills should be more robust than the description of the challenging behavior. The description of the student also borrowed information from the description of the challenging behavior but reframed it. Bouncing in her seat all day became "full of life and energy." Class clown became "creative and energetic." The power to see the positive is essential when developing a behavior plan, especially because you've already described the challenging behavior in the FBA.

The human brain is formed of three parts. The very back of the brain is the oldest part and it still functions as the fight or flight responder. The middle of the brain is the pleasure and pain center. The front of the brain is the thinking part of the brain, our executive functioning command center. The challenge is that all too often, the back and middle of the brain supersede the front of the brain and we are caught in a world of simply reacting to situations.

The fight or flight part of our brain is incredibly important for our survival, but it works overtime. It works so hard that sometimes we get caught up in just seeing what is wrong in the environment, where the danger is, and what could go awry that we forget to recalibrate and focus our brain on what is right and what could work perfectly. Safety and survival are important but most of the time we have the ability to shift our thoughts back to the front of our brain and focus on what is going well, what can go right, and what is good.

The behavior plan utilizes the information from the FBA to help focus everyone on the appropriate behavior. The goal is to connect the information from the assessment and then work toward identifying strengths, skills, and the appropriate behavior. Preparing the team to focus on what is right will assist in developing a plan that will foster the appropriate behavior and improve the classroom environment.

REFLECTION QUESTIONS

1. Describe a friend, spouse, co-worker, or family member using the birthday test. What are the strengths and skills that you included? Why?
2. What is a positive way to reframe the following:

   a. The student is off task.
   b. The student has no friends.
   c. The student is a grade level behind in reading.

Table 6.3. Completed Highlights of FBA

Sources of Information: (List sources of information used in FBA, both formal and informal, to develop this plan) Anecdotal teacher information; ABC data; interviews; frequency data; MAS and FAST
Strength-Based Profile (Identify skills and interests, positive relationships, prosocial behaviors, family and community supports, and other protective factors) *Sonya is full of life and energy. She has a strong desire to learn and interact with her peers. She loves her family and speaks of them often. She enjoys drawing, coloring, and crafting and often incorporates her two dogs into her art. Sonya thrives in a classroom that is structured and rulebound. She forms immediate bonds with adults. Sonya is able to participate in all classroom activities. Sonya enjoys leadership roles and being "the princess."*
Functional Behavioral Assessment (FBA) Summary Statement (Describe specific problem behavior and summary/hypothesis statement from FBA) When Sonya is on the playground or in unstructured settings with few adults, she will hit other students in order to gain attention from her peers as supported by ABC, baseline, and MAS/FAST data.

Chapter Seven

Chocolate for Almonds

Understanding the Functionally Equivalent Replacement Behavior (FERB) and Differentiation

You can't change how people treat you or what they say about you. All you can do is change how you react to it.

—*Mahatma Gandhi*

One of the first tricks to starting a weight loss or lifestyle change program is to address those pesky cravings. When you want salty chips, eat a little popcorn instead. When you are thirsty for a bubbly soda, try sparkling water. When your body is craving chocolate, eat a handful of almonds. Almonds? Yes. Your body craves foods because of the nutrients or lack of nutrients that it has. Believe it or not, when you are craving chocolate, it is most likely because you are deprived of magnesium, and many nuts are a rich source of the vitamin.

Understanding the functionally equivalent replacement behavior (FERB) is the same concept. The person is craving the outcome or the consequence, the function (that is, attention, escape). The goal is to find the functional equivalent, the healthy alternative. The FERB is the socially acceptable behavior that will garner the same outcome.

Many times the focus is so tuned in to the challenging behavior that it can be difficult to begin making the connection to the functionally equivalent

---

TEXTBOX 7.1.
Functionally Equivalent Replacement Behavior

Behavior that provides the same functional outcome in a socially appropriate manner.

55

behavior. For this reason, there is a need to focus on what is right. This is especially the case when jumping into the behavior planning without first reviewing the data and letting those data drive the decision making.

A person doesn't begin a new diet and give up chocolate without first understanding his or her current weight and lifestyle goals, right? In this case it is necessary to go back and review several of the components of the FBA to be sure the BIP is connected and aligned. The FBA is what drives the behavior planning.

FINDING THE FUNCTION

First, review all of the data including the ABC data, interviews, baseline data, and any tools used to help identify the function of the behavior. Pay close attention to the C column, the consequences, on the ABC data collection tool. Those are some of the data that helped to determine the function of the behavior and can give subtle hints to creating a FERB.

For instance, if the consequences were consistently about the teacher providing the student attention, such as teacher redirection, teacher reprimand, verbal warnings, etc., those can be clues as to how to shape a replacement behavior. If the consequences were consistently around getting out of doing something, like the student leaves the room or is in time out more than time in, that can be a FERB clue.

Also review the hypothesis statement and hypothesized function. Those will need to be tied directly to the replacement behavior. If the function is attention, the FERB will need to provide attention. If the function is tangible, the FERB will need to provide a tangible. The concept is the same as the almonds. If you are craving chocolate, it can't be replaced with potato chips.

Attention

Attention is one of the most common functions of behavior in the classroom. There is often strong competition in a classroom full of students to garner the direct attention of the teacher. Teachers are many times strong authoritarian figures that demand attention as the leaders of the classroom. Unfortunately, so many students are attention deprived and looking for opportunities to gain attention because attention often equates to social acceptance.

When the function of the behavior is hypothesized to be attention, the goal of the FERB is to find how the student can gain that attention in a positive manner. On the FBA, this is why attention is broken into adult and peer. The FERB is going to be different if the student is more often seeking adult attention or peer attention.

For a student that is seeking adult attention, the FERB will need to provide adult attention. To be even more specific, if the student is most often getting direct one-on-one attention from the teacher as a result of the challenging behavior, he or she should get that same kind of attention, if not more, for engaging in the socially appropriate behavior.

For example, a student is calling out answers out of turn and receiving attention from the teacher because the response is accepted. What is the socially appropriate way to get attention for knowing the right answer? Raising your hand and being called on. The FERB for calling out is to raise a quiet hand.

Behavior = calling out
FERB = raising a quiet hand

A student that is getting peer attention for telling jokes and acting silly in class is likely receiving that attention when students respond with laughter and social approval. Telling jokes and goofing off can be socially acceptable in the right setting, just not in the middle of a lesson or during independent work time. A FERB may be to schedule some joke telling time or some "silly time" so that peers can still respond but the timing is more appropriate.

Behavior = telling jokes during instruction or classwork time
FERB = telling jokes during approved "silly time"

Here are a few more examples of FERBs for attention.

FERB[1]

- Requesting attention/asking for help
- Classroom captain or jobs
- Contingent access to a preferred adult or peer
- Peer tutor/mentor
- Playing reciprocal games or turn taking practice
- Sharing strengths/skills with adults or peers
- Sharing work/art with adults or peers

Escape/Avoid

Escaping and avoiding difficult work or nonpreferred people are other common functions in the classroom setting. For many students the classroom can be a complicated environment to navigate. Students with deficits in academic and/or social skills areas may seek to remove themselves from those tasks or people.

Imagine the last time that you were in an overcrowded space or were asked to deliver a project in a tight timeline. There are times when it can feel overwhelming. Most of us have learned the skills to cope with and avoid or escape the situation in an appropriate manner. You can ask to be excused from the crowded space or simply and politely remove yourself. You can use techniques like taking a deep breath and knowing that you can enjoy a preferred activity if you stay for just twenty minutes to say hello to friends and colleagues.

You can organize your time appropriately so you only have to work on a task for small chunks of time or build in breaks. You can also learn to delegate or say no some projects. These are the same strategies that we want students to learn to utilize when the function is avoidance or escape.

> Behavior = doing other work than task assigned
> FERB = take small breaks after some work completed
>
> Behavior = running away due to loud noises
> FERB = put on headphones and take deep breaths

Here are some additional FERB strategies for avoidance and escape. Remember that avoidance means the challenging behavior allows the student to avoid starting the task while escape occurs once a task has begun.

FERB[2]

- Begin a task after a specific amount of time
- Request help or a break
- Request an alternative method of delivery (for example, oral, written, etc.); level of complexity (easy vs. difficult); order of delivery (first this then that)
- Remove or delay portions of task
- Use a visual or prompt to ask for assistance
- Learn social skills techniques to excuse self from challenging situations

Tangible

The function of tangible is about things. Things that are tangible are those items that you can hold. For younger students, tangibles are usually toys, games, stickers, etc. For older students, tangibles are often electronics, personal items, food, etc.

While all behavior is a form of communication, when it comes to tangible as a function, communication is key. Children often learn or are taught early on that if they ask nicely for an item, they will likely get access to it. Students that struggle with access to tangible items as a function have not yet learned to wait for their turn or ask for an item and wait until it is given to them.

The marshmallow experiment is a classic research study conducted in the 1960s.[3] It was structured around the concept of delayed gratification. Children were provided with some instructions from the researcher: essentially, eat a marshmallow now or wait and get two later. It is a game we often play with ourselves—engage in the behavior now, and it may have a benefit in the short term. Or wait and reap a larger benefit in the long term. The ability to wait one's turn is a valuable development skill, but one that not all children may have mastered yet. This is why it is important to consider teaching communication and wait skills.

Behavior = grabbing toy away from another child
FERB = asking another child for permission to play with toy

Here are several simple FERBs for tangible.

FERB[4]

- Ask politely for item
- Raise hand and ask for item
- Accept an alternative item
- Wait a specified amount of time to receive access to item

Sensory

Sensory is probably the trickiest function to understand. Therefore it's difficult for most to conceptualize how to access the function of sensory appropriately. Sensory has to do with physical stimulation. Think of your five senses: sight, sound, smell, touch, taste. These are connected to the function of sensory.

The challenging behavior most often comes when a person is either deprived of or overstimulated by one or more of the senses. It is important to ask if this sensation would happen if no one was around, if the person were in a room void of anything. Consider if you were in an empty room and you stubbed your toe. It may hurt a bit, but likely your behavior would be different if there was someone else in the room with you. You may exaggerate the pain to gain a bit of sympathy. The pain is still there, but because a person is present, the behavior of shouting out loud is more likely for the attention.

For a person that exhibits challenging behavior for the function of sensory stimulation, his or her response would be exaggerated even if no one was around. Common sensory behaviors can include things like rocking, flapping, fidgeting, tearing items, putting pressure on body parts, and repetitive behaviors.

Behavior = hitting self on leg
FERB = place hands in pocket

Here some other ideas to address sensory FERBs.

FERB[5]

- Use of a fidget toy (squeeze ball, spinner, worry stone)
- Sitting on hands or hands in pockets
- Weighted blanket or stuffed animal in lap
- Clay, putty, dough to roll and squeeze
- Deep breathing techniques
- Aromatherapy
- Chewing gum/candy
- Exercise breaks
- Proprioceptive activities (jumping jacks, pushups, running, etc.)

A FERB is an opportunity for a student to gain the same function or outcome, but because he or she has engaged in the appropriate behavior instead of the inappropriate behavior. He or she has decided to eat the healthy almond instead of the ooey-gooey brownie chocolate bar. The FERB is not just the opposite of the challenging behavior either; it has to serve the same function. The FERB is developed thoughtfully and with data determining the socially appropriate behavior, which will provide the same function. When the student is engaging in the appropriate behavior, there is less of a reason to engage in the challenging behavior.

REFLECTION QUESTIONS

1. If you have a student who tends to get out of his or her seat or area and touches other students' personal items, what could be a possible replacement behavior?
2. Think about your own behaviors. Is there a habit that you have that some might consider challenging or unhealthy, for example, biting your nails or chewing loudly? What is a replacement behavior for your challenging behavior?
3. How could you help a colleague to understand why a FERB is important?

Table 7.1. Completed FERB

Functionally Equivalent Replacement Behavior (Behavior that provides the same functional outcome in a socially appropriate manner)
• Murray will request a two-minute time away when he feels anxious, upset, or frustrated.

NOTES

1. Adapted from Sonoma County CA, SELPA for PENT Forums; Escambia County Schools Behavior Intervention Guide.

2. Adapted from Sonoma County CA, SELPA for PENT Forums; Escambia County Schools Behavior Intervention Guide.

3. W. Mischel, E. B. Ebbesen, and A. R. Zeiss, "Cognitive and Attentional Mechanisms in Delay of Gratification," *Journal of Personality and Social Psychology* 21, no. 2 (February 1972): 204–18.

4. Adapted from Sonoma County CA, SELPA for PENT Forums; Escambia County Schools Behavior Intervention Guide.

5. Adapted from Sonoma County CA, SELPA for PENT Forums; Escambia County Schools Behavior Intervention Guide.

Chapter Eight

Strategies to Decrease Behavior

It is easier to build strong children than to repair broken adults.

—*Frederick Douglass*

Imagine having a beautiful home beside a creek. Days are spent sitting on the back porch watching the calm water trickle down over the river rocks. The water is clean. Animals come to the edge to drink and bathe. Flowers and trees reach their roots into the pristine waters.

While sitting one day, watching the rippled waves move past the banks of the creek, you notice a piece of trash floating in the creek. The water is normally crystal clear. Before long, several more pieces of litter are seen on top of the water.

You walk to the edge of the creek and collect as much of the trash as you can, satisfied that the creek is still immaculate. When walking back to the house, you notice more trash floating in the water. You attempt to collect as much as possible, but there is already too much in your arms from the earlier collection. You gather even more and are saddened that the creek is still full of trash and you can't gather it all before sundown.

The next day you quickly walk to the edge of the creek only to see that the water is jammed with garbage. It is far too much for one person to clean up. While talking to a neighbor, he mentions that a big new attraction was built several miles up the creek and so many people have visited it lately, it must be where all the litter is coming from.

This sparks an idea. Rather than spend all day trying to clean up the garbage, you go up the river to try to stop the litter from being thrown in the creek. You and your neighbors create signs to help remind people to use the garbage bins, you have the owners of the new attraction install more garbage bins and a fence along the water, and you thank people that are seen throwing trash in the receptacles.

Now you sit on the porch again and enjoy the calm soothing waters and gentle breeze through the cattails. Once in a while you'll see a small piece of litter in the water that can be scooped up and thrown away.

Prevention strategies do work. Benjamin Franklin said that an ounce of prevention is worth a pound of cure. The concept of prevention is just as important in the classroom. It is better to arrange the environment to avoid or remove the need for the challenging behavior than to wait for the challenging behavior and then respond. The latter creates a classroom that is reactive.

As a teacher, a majority of the day is spent responding to crisis and concern rather than instruction. In the classroom, just like in the creek, it is important to consider the impact of our actions. If enough time isn't spent setting up a strong classroom management system (the litter bins and fences) and preparing in advance for behavioral challenges, then a great deal of time in the classroom is likely going to be spent trying to address garbage behaviors.

If it feels like most of the day is spent putting out fires, then it is time to focus on strategies to prevent challenging behavior. There are two opportunities to reduce challenging classroom behaviors before they begin: making adjustments to the setting events that may increase the likelihood of the behavior occurring and antecedent manipulations. Thus, making changes to what happens just before the challenging behavior.

Table 8.1.   Setting Events and Antecedents

Setting Event Strategies *(Reduce impact of setting events)*	**Antecedent Strategies** *(Decrease likelihood that behavior will occur)*

SETTING EVENTS

Remember from the data collection and analysis process that antecedents are the events that happen immediately before a challenging behavior. Setting events are what happen before the antecedent that may make the behavior more or less likely to occur. They have a kind of symbiotic relationship. Consider the following scenarios.

Your alarm did not go off in the morning; you are running late for work. You aren't able to stop at your favorite coffee shop on the way in to work. When you arrive, your administrator is in the office and looks at her watch, noting the time you arrived. Your classroom door is jammed and you can't find the facilities manager to let you in. A colleague asks how you are doing and you begin to curse and rant about how terrible your morning has been up to this point.

There are a number of setting events that lead to what some might consider the challenging behavior of cursing at your peer. Let's take a closer look.

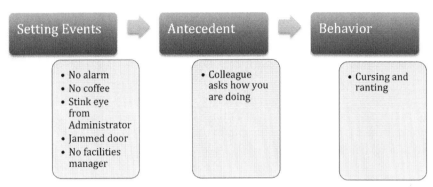

Figure 8.1.   Setting Events

On most days one or two things may occur in the morning and the day is just fine. Some mornings are probably sunshine and roses. But on that particular morning, there were a number of setting events that created the perfect storm and altered the typical behavior toward a peer's question.

Consider a classroom example. Sonya has a hard time sleeping at night. Her family has tried earlier bedtimes, lavender oil, even warm milk, but Sonya has only been getting three to four hours of sleep per night. In the mornings, she has several siblings that require a great deal of attention from her parents. The car ride to school is often loud.

When Sonya arrives at school, she sees her classmates talking and playing with each other. Sonya is not invited into the groupings and is often isolated from her peers. The classroom is also noisy and can be distracting. When students are asked to participate in group work, Sonya is typically not picked by her peers. When the students are all together on the playground, Sonya wants to play games with her peers.

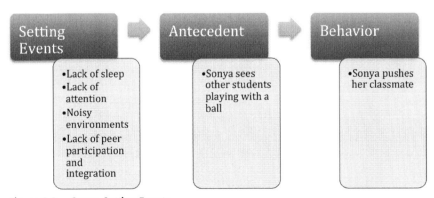

Figure 8.2.   Sonya Setting Events

There are events that occur in our lives that may make an antecedent more powerful. Setting events are often called triggers because they trigger an antecedent differently. There are often a number of triggers in our lives. The goal when changing behavior is to either address the triggers or the response to the triggers.

The best case scenario would be for you to double check the alarm clock before bed or ensure that Sonya has a good eight hours of sleep each night. But triggers are often out of our control or they happen without being able to adjust. There is little that the teacher can do about Sonya's life outside of the classroom. The teacher can't be there at night to help her get enough sleep or be in the car in the mornings to keep the noise level down and pay attention to Sonya.

So the next best scenario is to control the environment to help reduce the impact of setting events. For Sonya, knowing that she may be tired in the morning and overstimulated, the expectation for the classroom could be a quiet bell work activity to help everyone acclimate. Sonya could begin the day with a Social Story[1] about making friends in which she learns skills to interact with peers. The first classroom activity could be a paired activity in which Sonya is partnered with a compassionate peer. Sonya could have a break built into the morning to provide her some rest or additional time to practice social skills.

By arranging the environment based on understanding what the triggers are, there may be less likelihood that when Sonya sees the other students playing with the ball outside she will become aggressive. If the triggers are reduced and all those additional opportunities to learn appropriate responses are available, there is less need for the challenging behavior.

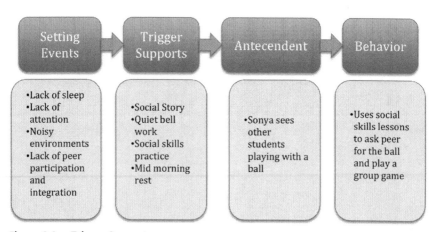

Figure 8.3.   Trigger Supports

BEFORE THE BEHAVIOR

Another strategy is to address the actual antecedent event. This is especially useful when possible triggers are unknown because a pattern hasn't been established or the triggers are unclear. This is also helpful when there is simply no way to manage the triggers.

The antecedent is the event that occurs immediately before the challenging behavior, typically within thirty seconds. Think back to the ABC data collection process. The A is the place that prevention can occur, and antecedent manipulation is a powerful strategy.

Changing the antecedent can either decrease the likelihood of the challenging behavior or even increase the likelihood of the *preferred* behavior. The next chapter will share more tips on increasing the preferred behavior. For now, the focus is on decreasing the challenging behavior.

In the earlier example, the antecedent is the presence of the ball in the possession of a peer. For Sonya, it is less about wanting the ball and more about wanting to play with her classmates. To change the antecedent, the teacher could work with the classmate to present the ball to Sonya and ask her to play. This changes the antecedent from Sonya seeing other students playing with the ball to Sonya being asked to play with other students and the ball.

Understanding the triggers and antecedents will allow for prevention of the challenging behavior. Prevention is about setting up the environment to favor the appropriate or preferred behavior rather than the challenging behavior. Consider that if the fish in an aquarium are unhealthy, it makes more sense to treat the water and clean up the aquarium than to scoop each fish out and try to treat each individually. Setting up the classroom for success is the best strategy. Chapter 9 will offer more tips for antecedent manipulation that will increase the likelihood of the FERB and the preferred behaviors.

REFLECTION QUESTIONS

1. After reading about Murray in previous chapters, what would be the setting events and possible antecedents that are impacting his challenging behavior?
2. What do you do when setting events or triggers impact your daily routine? What are your coping strategies?
3. What is one immediate change that you could make in the classroom tomorrow that would help to address setting events for one or more students?

Table 8.2. Completed Setting Events and Antecedents

Setting Event Strategies *(Reduce impact of setting events)*	**Antecedent Strategies** *(Decrease likelihood that behavior will occur)*
• Social Story • Quiet bell work • Social skills practice • Mid-morning rest	• Teach peers to share • Teach Sonya to request items or playtime with peers • Schedule peer-to-peer playtime during recess/organize play

NOTE

1. C. Gray and J. Garand, "Social Stories: Improving Responses of Individuals with Autism with Accurate Social Information," *Focus on Autistic Behavior* 8 (1993): 1–10.

Chapter Nine

What Is Caught Should Be Taught

Strategies to Teach and Reinforce Behavior

An old Cherokee told his grandson, "my son, there is a battle between two wolves inside us all. One is evil. It is anger, jealousy, greed, resentment, inferiority, lies, and ego. The other is good. It is joy, peace, love, hope, humility, kindness, empathy, and truth." He thought about it and asked, "grandfather, which wolf wins?" The old man quietly replied, "the one you feed."

—Anonymous

A teacher's day is spent facilitating instruction. Teachers are continually evaluated on the level and effectiveness of instruction. Academic lesson plans include instruction across multiple subject areas or across topics in a single subject area. Students are tested on how well they have absorbed and comprehended the instruction. There is a strong desire in education to understand the impact of teaching on student outcomes.

However, there is rarely the same effort and expectation to teach *behavior* to the same degree that we teach academics. In actuality, academics are behaviors. Writing is a behavior. Reading is a behavior. Calculating fractions is a behavior. Social skills are behavior. Emotional regulation is behavior. Initiating conversations with a peer is behavior. Even raising a quiet hand is a behavior. And they all have to be taught.

Once a replacement behavior has been determined, it has to be taught. The replacement behavior has to be taught and reinforced with the same intensity, frequency, and duration—if not more—than the challenging behavior. It has to be taught and then it has to be caught.

Table 9.1. FERB and Reinforcement Strategies

FERB Behavior Strategies Increase the likelihood that the appropriate replacement behavior will occur through instruction
•
Reinforcement of the FERB Strategies Consequence
•

It was explained in chapter 8 that there are multiple strategies that can be used to prevent challenging behaviors: before the behavior occurs, manipulating the antecedent, or after the behavior occurs, manipulating the consequence. Prevention is typically the best medicine, but a strong BIP also addresses consequence strategies.

When determining a consequence strategy, the first step is to understand how manipulating a consequence can impact the behavior. There are two main types of consequence strategies: reinforcement and punishment.

Reinforcement is either adding something or taking something away from the environment in an effort to increase the likelihood of a behavior continuing in the future. Punishment is adding or removing something from the environment to decrease the likelihood of the behavior occurring in the future. The difference is in the impact to the behavior, the outcome. Both procedures can either be positive, adding a stimulus or event, or negative, removing a stimulus or event.

Table 9.2. Positive and Negative Consequences

	Positive +	Negative −
Reinforcement	Adding something to the environment to *increase* the likelihood of the behavior	Removing something from the environment to *increase* the likelihood of the behavior
Punishment	Adding something to the environment to *decrease* the likelihood of the behavior	Removing something from the environment to *decrease* the likelihood of the behavior

Adapted from *Happy Class: The Practical Guide for Classroom Management.*

BRING IN THE REINFORCEMENTS

The most common mistake that is often heard is the confusion of negative reinforcement and punishment. There is an important difference. Think back to the data collection process and the ABC data. The C column is where the pattern of the consequence was identified. There were likely some consequences that occurred often and perhaps a few that only occurred once or twice. The consequences that occurred over and over were the reinforcers for the challenging behavior. Why? If the behavior continued to occur, something was either being added or removed from the environment to increase or maintain the behavior.

That is the consequence test. It can only be concluded if something is a reinforcer or punisher by what happens to the challenging behavior. If the behavior continues, something is reinforcing it. If the behavior decreases then something is acting as a punisher.

If you focus too much on the weeds in the garden, the flowers will not grow strong. When developing the BIP, the focus is on teaching the appropriate behavior and ensuring that the FERB is reinforced, making the replacement behavior more likely to occur in the future. There are multiple types of reinforcement that can be utilized to encourage that appropriate behavior. But first, the student must learn the new skill.

There are two assumptions that can be made. One, the student does not know how to engage in the appropriate behavior (that is, can't do). Two, the inappropriate behavior is so powerfully reinforced, it's worth it to the student to get in trouble (that is, won't do).

Consider Murray and his disruptive classroom behavior. He is behaving like a class clown to get attention. Clearly he gets a reaction from the teacher. That reaction is maintaining that challenging behavior. The teacher and other adults in the area likely respond to the behavior by reprimanding Murray, reminding him about the rules, and commenting to him about his behavior. Joking around and being loud in the classroom works well for Murray; he gets a big reaction from his teacher.

Thinking about the two assumptions, there is an opportunity to teach Murray an appropriate replacement behavior and also provide reinforcement that is more potent than the big reaction he is currently getting from adults. In other words, the reinforcement for using the FERB should come from his teacher and have just as big of a reaction.

Consider if you are really hungry and sitting in front of you is a bowl of hearty, thick soup inside a locked box. Next to that is a single uncooked pea inside another locked box. Most people are going to want to eat the hearty soup. But to eat the soup, you first must figure out—learn or be taught—how to unlock the box. Then you'll have the sustenance that you need.

This part of the BIP follows the same logic. A tip is to go into the process believing that if the student is engaging in the challenging behavior, he or she has not yet learned the skill he or she needs to replace that behavior. Even if the student should have developmentally learned the skill at some point in his or her life, if the student is not *using* the skill, a first step should always be to teach the replacement behavior. Teach first, then reward the use of the new skill. Teach, teach, teach. Reinforce, reinforce, reinforce.

Another important tidbit is that behavior is communication and in most cases a sound place to begin is teaching what needs to be communicated more effectively. In Sonya's case, she needs to learn how to communicate to her peers that she wants their attention. A strategy may be to teach her to introduce herself to a classmate and request something.

Attention from peers (function) → *social skills training (teaching)* → *peer interaction (consequence/reinforce)*

Once Sonya has learned the new skill of introducing herself and making a request, like asking to play a game, the peer will need to provide the reinforcement. And that reinforcement will need to be *big*. Part of the learning process should be peers and classmates working with Sonya to learn the new skill and creating different ways to congratulate her for using it like high fives, loud claps, class cheers, access to the best toy, or a group game. There are social skills programs that can help to teach specific skills that may be necessary. Examples are programs such as Skillstreaming,[1] PATHS,[2] or Prepare.[3] With a simple online keyword search, additional social skills strategies can also be found easily online.

For Murray's behavior, he may need to learn when it is okay to be loud and make jokes with friends. Teach him when there are unstructured times when he can engage with his peers. Teach his peers the times that they can interact and joke around with Murray and when they may need to ignore some of his inappropriate behavior.

Ignoring inappropriate behavior is a valuable strategy that can be used when the function is attention. The strategy has to be planned. The MDT will want to consider the impact of planning strategically to ignore some attention-seeking behavior. Ignoring challenging behavior can create what is referred to as an extinction burst. This means that the challenging behavior will likely get worse before it gets better.

The key is to treat the teaching of the replacement behavior like any other subject area. There may be lesson plans that are developed for the use of a specific training or program. There will need to be time set aside for instructional delivery and practice. There may need to be some whole and small group instruction as well as the individual instruction. The skill will need to be taught in different modalities and based on the learner's need.

Students may need to learn social skills. They may need to learn how to wait for an item. They may need to learn how to communicate a need or how to self-soothe. The skill being taught is going to align with the FERB.

Several common or recommended behavioral teaching strategies are described in table 9.3.

Table 9.3. Teaching Strategies

Behavioral Teaching Strategy	Description
Shaping*	The process of reinforcing successive approximations of the behavior until the end goal is met. Requires that overall behavior be broken into more finite steps. Each step is taught or naturally occurs and is reinforced until the full chain of behaviors is completed together. Best for complex behaviors that can be chunked into smaller tasks (for example, teaching toileting or language development).
Prompting*	Providing visual, sound, or touch prompts to cue the occurrence or need for a specific behavior and the steps to accomplish the behavior. Prompting is like a recipe card for the correct behavior.
Behavioral Momentum*	Utilizes simpler requests or actions/behaviors the student can easily accomplish followed by more complicated behaviors. The easy behaviors build up to the more complicated behavior. Example: Easy-easy-easy-more difficult-easy-easy-more difficult-easy-more difficult-easy-more difficult-done!
Social Stories**	Create personalized stories that simplify and teach the necessary skills to engage in appropriate behavior. Can be created using clip art images or personal photos of the student practicing the behavior. Social stories can vary in length and complexity based on developmental level and age. Multiple social stories can be created to teach a variety of behaviors.
Error Corrections*	Utilizing teachable moments to correct the challenging behavior and reteach the appropriate behavior. Overcorrection is also a procedure that has the student practice the appropriate behavior multiple times. Example: If a student runs in the hallway, he or she may be asked to return to the classroom and walk appropriately.

(continued)

Table 9.3. *Continued*

Communication Training*	Teaching effective verbal, signing, or visual image communication strategies. Students may learn simple one-word requests or more complex patterns of communication. Electronic tools or picture exchange tools may be used to assist with verbal communication.

*John O. Cooper, Timothy E. Heron, and William L. Heward, *Applied Behavior Analysis* (Upper Saddle River, NJ: Pearson/Merrill-Prentice Hall, 2007).
**C. Gray and J. Garand, "Social Stories: Improving Responses of Individuals with Autism with Accurate Social Information," *Focus on Autistic Behavior* 8 (1993): 1–10.

TEACHING BEHAVIOR

During the teaching process, the reinforcement strategies will need to be in place. The process of learning should include acknowledgment of the appropriate behavior and encouragement to continue to use the FERB. The replacement behavior will provide access to the function (a FERB of raising a quiet hand will produce attention from an adult), but there is typically still a need for some extra encouragement.

There are different types of reinforcement procedures that may help to address the use of the FERB. These are often referred to as differential reinforcement procedures. This is just a fancy way of saying that a different behavior than the challenging behavior is going to be reinforced. Table 9.4 shows different types of reinforcement strategies and brief descriptions.

Table 9.4. **Differential Reinforcement Strategies**

DRA Differential Reinforcement of Alternative/Appropriate Behaviors	Reinforcing the alternative or appropriate behavior (FERB) Example: When the student becomes frustrated by a difficult assignment, he or she is taught to use a signal to request a break. The student is allowed to take a five-minute break and earns a sticker on a chart.
DRI Differential Reinforcement of Incompatible Behaviors	Reinforcing a behavior that is incompatible with the challenging behavior Example: When the student is unable to keep his or her hands to his- or herself at the table, he or she is taught to keep his or her hands on top of the table placed on two stickers shaped like hands so they are visible. When he or she keeps his or her hands on the stickers for five minutes, he or she earns a high five from each of his or her table partners and the teacher and gets a handful of cereal bits.

DRL Differential Reinforcement of Lower Rates of Behaviors	Reinforcing a lower rate of a challenging behavior (typically a nonaggressive, minimally disruptive behavior) Example: When the student calls out in class, it can occur up to ten times during an hour. The teacher determined that two times per hour is more typical for the other students in the class. The student is taught that when he or she only calls out twice per hour, he or she will earn five minutes of one-on-one time with the teacher.
DRO Differential Reinforcement of Other Behaviors	Reinforcing the nonoccurrence of the behavior during a specified period of time. Example: When the student gets out of his or her seat and wanders the classroom, it can be distracting and dangerous. For the next few weeks the student will earn a token for each twenty-minute period he or she sits in his or her seat and completes classwork or participates with peers. The tokens can be traded for a no homework pass at the end of the week.

*John O. Cooper, Timothy E. Heron, and William L. Heward, *Applied Behavior Analysis* (Upper Saddle River, NJ: Pearson/Merrill-Prentice Hall, 2007).

The replacement behavior needs to be taught through sound instructional practices. The replacement behavior also needs to be caught and reinforced. The goal of this part of the BIP is to begin to transition the students' need to engage in the challenging behavior with a more socially appropriate and age appropriate behavior.

The plan for teaching and reinforcing should be detailed enough to pass the substitute test. If a substitute were in the classroom, would he or she know what to do to help teach and reinforce the replacement behavior? The plan should be detailed in a way that other professional staff would know what to do and when. This is really the heart of the BIP. This is the component of the BIP that helps to create a better quality of life for the student and teaches the skills necessary for long-term success.

REFLECTION QUESTIONS

1. Negative reinforcement is removing an aversive stimulus from the environment to increase the likelihood a behavior will occur again in the future. An example is removing rain from falling in your face by putting up an umbrella. The next time it rains, you'll be more likely to open an umbrella. What is a classroom example of negative reinforcement?

2. A student is struggling with an academic skill and often avoids the work by talking with her peers. How could you use each of the differential reinforcement strategies to address the challenging behavior?
3. You are working on teaching a student how to keep his hands and feet to himself in the hallways. You want to use either a social story or error correction. Which would you choose and why?
4. Larry struggles to interact appropriately with his peers. He is in middle school and is fairly new to the school. He is able to initiate conversation but not able to maintain conversations with peers. His classmates often call him "weird" or "strange." You want to help him make friends and interact in an age appropriate manner. Search online for social skills programs or lessons that would address his unique needs. What were you able to find?

Table 9.5.   Completed FERB and Reinforcement Strategies

FERB Behavior Strategies Increase the likelihood that the appropriate replacement behavior will occur through instruction
• Sonya will be taught to initiate conversation with peers • Staff will utilize a peer-to-peer social skills program • Sonya will have twenty minutes each morning to read a Social Story about peer-to-peer interaction • After the Social Story, Sonya will choose one peer to practice with for ten minutes • On the playground, Sonya will be partnered with a student buddy who will help to initiate peer-to-peer conversation • Sonya may only utilize equipment or toys that she has asked appropriately for; classmates have been taught to say, "not right now, Sonya, please ask nicely" • Sonya, will be prompted/reminded to initiate conversation by saying, "hi, I'm interested in that, can I play?" or "hi, I'd like to join, may I?"
Reinforcement of the FERB Strategies Consequence
• When Sonya appropriately initiates conversation with her classmates, she can earn a sticker • Each sticker is worth one minute of additional free time with a preferred peer at the end of the day • Sonya also earns a bonus sticker each morning for completing her Social Story practice appropriately • She can earn up to ten stickers a day (based on baseline data)

NOTES

1. E. McGinnis and A. P. Goldstein, *Skillstreaming the Elementary School Child: New Strategies and Perspectives for Teaching Prosocial Skills* (Champaign, IL: Research Press, 1997).

2. C. A. Kusche and M. T. Greenberg, *PATHS: Promoting Alternative Thinking Strategies* (South Deerfield, MA: Channing-Bete, 1997).

3. A. P. Goldstein, *The Prepare Curriculum: Teaching Prosocial Competencies* (Champaign, IL: Research Press, 1999).

Chapter Ten

Strategies to Increase Integrity and Generalization of Implementation

You can't force a seed to grow by being frustrated with it . . . but you can help it grow by watering it regularly.

—Anonymous

A completed plan has been developed. All the pieces have come together for a cohesive plan. From the beginning of data collection, through hypothesizing the function, to developing an intervention plan, a team of professional educators has collaborated to create a system of support for a student. Now is the time to determine how to maintain the plan and ensure its success.

The greatest challenge of any plan is sticking to it. Going back to the idea of a diet, the first week may be a breeze because it's new and fresh; it's something different. There is a collection of all of the newest trendy tips and recipes. After a few months, however, there is a tendency to drift back to old habits and not maintain consistency. It is easier to choose the pizza after a busy day than to prep a week's worth of healthy salads. However, that won't help you stay on track toward the goal of losing weight!

The BIP can be very similar. In the beginning staff may be excited to try new strategies and see some quick change. People are likely desperate for something different after handling challenging behaviors for a period of time. But after a while, people typically revert to their previous habits and lose sight of the behavior goals.

Table 10.1. Behavior Intervention Plan

Evaluation and Continuous Progress Monitoring Method:		Person Responsible:	
Criterion for Success:		Follow-Up Meeting Date:	
Contextual Fit (Supports, resources, and training needed for personnel to implement this plan in the current/most likely setting)		•	
Generalization (Supports, resources, and training needed for personnel to implement this plan across multiple settings)		•	
Communicating the Behavior Intervention Plan			
Person to be contacted:	How contact will be made:	Person responsible for contact:	Date/frequency of contact:
Who will communicate revisions and updates internally and externally?			

Here is something to help put it into perspective. For each year that the person has engaged in the challenging behavior, it may take that many months of consistent implementation of a plan to make significant change. In other words, if the student is eleven years old and he or she had challenges with keeping his or her hands to him- or herself for as long as can be remembered, it will take nearly a year of *consistent* implementation of a behavior change plan to reduce the challenging behavior to an acceptable level.

So when staff say, "we tried that behavior stuff; it never works!" Ask, "Is it because the behavior intervention plan was never implemented consistently and fully?" When staff or families feel that there needs to be an immediate change in the behavior, remind them that it is going to take time and effort to make a change. This is especially the case if there is an extinction burst and the behavior becomes more challenging temporarily. Rome wasn't built in a day and no one loses twenty pounds in one day!

Consistency is also key. The plan will need to be communicated, shared, taught, and implemented in a way that ensures consistency of implementation. Students are the first to recognize which teacher or staff member they can get away with something and they realize when a plan is not being implemented consistently. From very young students to high schoolers, they quickly learn the loopholes. They learn with who they can get away with what.

One strategy is to create an easy to read one-page implementation guide. They can even be laminated so that staff can easily carry them around the school. This one-page guide should have any relevant student information, the function of the behavior, the ongoing data collection method, and the important intervention components of the implementation plan.

Table 10.2.   One-Page Intervention Tool

Student Name:					Initial Date of Plan:	
Teacher:						
Function:						
Data Collection (Event Recording)						
1st period						
2nd period						
3rd period						
Lunch						
4th period						
5th period						
Bus lot						
Intervention Plan:						
•						
•						
•						

COLLABORATING FOR SUCCESS

When each teacher and staff member interacts with the student and is armed with the right information to support the plan, there is a better chance for implementation success. Each person will need to have training and coaching on how to implement the plan, what to look for to reinforce the appropriate behavior(s), and what to do when the challenging behavior occurs. It can't be assumed that staff will know what to do just because they have the plan in their hands. Create time for training and feedback on the implementation plan.

Once staff have had initial training on the plan, it is also important to provide additional coaching. If there are support staff as part of the MDT that are assisting with the plan development, they may be a good resource to support ongoing training and coaching while the teaching staff implement the plan. It is a team effort!

The other important part to successful implementation of a plan is something called generalization. Imagine that it is time to learn how to drive a car. The person teaching asks the student driver to sit on the couch and proceeds to place two cans of beans on the ground and a hat in the driver's hands. The cans of beans represent the brake and acceleration pedals and the hat is the steering wheel.

The trainer gives all the important and necessary information to learn how to drive and a great deal of time is spent practicing with the beans and hat. All of the skills have been mastered to pass the driving test except what? Actually practicing out on the road! The assumption is that the skills learned on the couch will apply on the road, and that isn't usually the case.

Similarly, if a student only practices the behavior in the same classroom, with the same peers or teacher, there is no guarantee that he or she will know how to use the behavior in a new setting or with different people. The skill has to be taught through generalization. The goal is for the replacement behavior, the appropriate behavior, to be practiced and reinforced in a safe learning environment until fluent, and then the skill should to be taught and reinforced in a variety of settings with a variety of people, another reason it is so important to have everyone that interacts with the student trained.

To help generalize behaviors, pay attention to the data. Because data are being collected continuously throughout the plan, it will be visible when the behavior has leveled out. In other words, when the data of the replacement behavior are consistent, it is probably time to consider practicing the behavior in another setting and/or with new people. This can be done until the student can easily and consistently utilize the replacement behavior across multiple settings and people.

FADING FOR THE FUTURE

The other step to consider once the student is regularly and successfully using the replacement behavior across settings is to begin to fade the reinforcer.

There is a common misperception that reinforcing behavior creates a reliance on external rewards.[1] That misconception is because people don't create fading plans for their overall goals. The goal of a successful intervention plan is that at some point it has been implemented so well that it is no longer needed, and that includes reducing the ongoing regular reinforcement.

To fade reinforcement literally means to reduce how often the replacement behavior is reinforced. Remember the DRL? Essentially, the data will indicate when the replacement behavior is consistently being used by the student. Once there is consistency, the reinforcer can be decreased slightly. If the behavior was being reinforced every time it occurred, change it to every other time. There may be a slight bump in the road at first, but be consistent and utilize the data to indicate if it is working or not. If the student is not successful, go back to the previous reinforcement schedule until the data are consistent and try it again.

The goal is to gradually fade or reduce the reinforcement until the student is engaging in the replacement behavior with no additional external rewards. Again, this may take a long time and will require consistent implementation, but the reward for the student in the long run is a better quality of life! There are also instances when a student may always need to be on a plan, his or her behavior is so severe, or he or she requires that layer of ongoing support, and that is okay too. Find the balance of implementation by utilizing the data. The data should always indicate consistency with little variation in the data points. The data should look like a smooth path rather than a mountain range.

TRAINING THE TEAM

Finally, an important piece to consider is who to train and include in the plan. There may be up to hundreds of people that the student will interact with during a single day. Do all of them have to be trained? Do all of them have to be experts? Not usually. Most of the time, if the main support staff and MDT are trained they can assist with the daily implementation.

For example, the members of the MDT who are highly knowledgeable of the plan can implement the majority of the plan across the school settings and across the day. The ancillary staff members that the student interacts with may also need additional training and support. Think about everyone the student interacts with who would be most likely to see the challenging behavior and the replacement behavior. Common people that may need additional training are

- bus drivers,
- hallway monitors,

- cafeteria staff,
- specials/electives teachers,
- front office staff,
- classroom volunteers,
- administration staff,
- substitute staff (if available), and
- instructional assistants.

There is a saying that most people don't plan to fail, they fail to plan. This is especially true with behavior plans. The only behavior you can truly control is your own! The responsibility of adjusting to the plan and ensuring successful implementation is yours. The goal is to set up the environment through training, support, and reinforcement so that the plan is able to be easily implemented, but if something isn't working, don't give up. It just means that the team needs to come back to the table and consider adjustments.

The BIP should be a fluid document. It should be calibrated, adjusted, and modified as necessary and based on the data. It is okay to make tweaks to the plan. In fact, it is best to use the data throughout the process to determine what is working and not working, make changes, and review the data again after the changes are implemented.

There may even be times when the team needs to look back at the FBA portion of the plan. Typically, the team should review the full plan at least once a year but can certainly review the FBA and BIP more than once a year. In the beginning, the team should be reviewing the impact of the BIP at least weekly. That can be spread out once the plan is being implemented consistently and data are indicating the student is consistently responding positively to the behavior plan. Successful teams create a calendar of check-ins and hold each other accountable for meeting regularly.

Table 10.3 shows some of the common areas that may need to be adjusted and some problem solving to assist.

Table 10.3.   Troubleshooting Ideas

Troubleshooting	Consider This
Student is not responding and utilizing the replacement behavior	• Adjust the schedule of reinforcement. • Is the replacement behavior aligned to the hypothesized function? • Is the hypothesized function accurate?
Student is more often engaging in the challenging behavior	• Is the reinforcement for the replacement behavior "strong" enough? • Is the replacement behavior being reinforced consistently?

Troubleshooting	Consider This
Staff are not utilizing the plan	• Is a refresher training needed? • Do staff need additional reinforcement to engage in the plan (for example, thank you notes, additional time to plan, etc.)? • Do staff need feedback on their implementation of the plan?
Student no longer responds to reinforcer	• Is the external reward preferred by the student? Conduct an interest inventory to find out what may function as a reinforcement. • Is the schedule of reinforcement too loose or too tight? • Has the "newness" worn off? Try a strategy like a mystery motivator to increase the interest.
No data, inaccurate or minimal data are being collected	• Is the data collection system too complex? Create a simpler data collection tool. • Is the data collection tool portable and easy to carry? • Is everyone trained to collect data? • Is a refresher training needed on data collection?
Peers/classmates are not consistently implementing the plan	• Is a refresher training needed? • Are there incentives/rewards for peers/classmates?
The replacement behavior is not generalizing to other settings	• Is enough practice time allocated to other settings? • Is there time dedicated to practice the behavior with others in a different settings? • Are staff trained to provide reinforcement in other settings? • Is it too soon to begin generalizing to other settings?
Student quickly mastered replacement behavior	• Do the data show the challenging behavior decreasing *and* the replacement behavior increasing or maintaining? • Was the replacement behavior aligned to the function? • Can a new replacement behavior also be taught?

*G. Thomas Schanding Jr. and Heather E. Sterling-Turner, "Use of the Mystery Motivator for a High School Class," *Journal of Applied School Psychology* 26, no. 1 (2010): 38–53.

The BIP process may take some trial and error. It may take several iterations before the right function aligns with the right strategies and the right strategies align with the right reward. Stay optimistic. Use the data. Focus on consistency. Work collaboratively as a team. And remember, the goal of the entire process is to create an environment in which the student can be successful and *happy*.

REFLECTION QUESTIONS

1. You notice that the student is using the replacement behavior of requesting a break consistently in all settings but one. When the team reviews the data, they notice that the student is still engaging in the challenging behavior more often in math class. What are questions that you may ask to troubleshoot?
2. The student struggles most in unstructured settings such as the hallway during transition times. There is not a staff member that is consistently available to monitor those unstructured times. What are some other solutions the team could consider?
3. Evan is a quick learner. The team implemented a plan to address the function of attention and taught Evan to put a green notecard on the corner of his desk when he wanted the teacher's attention or had a question. Evan mastered that skill; however, he is not using the notecard in Mrs. Daughtry's classroom. What are some things to consider?

Table 10.4. Behavior Intervention Plan

Evaluation and Continuous Progress Monitoring Method: Frequency data Monitored weekly by core MDT Share with family monthly	Person Responsible: Data collection: classroom teacher Data graphing: social worker Weekly meetings: classroom teacher Monthly meetings: school psychologist
Criterion for Success: Sonya will interact with peers and maintain appropriate conversation without physical or verbal aggression 90 percent of all observed occasions within eight weeks.	Follow-Up Meeting Date: January 7, 2019

Contextual Fit (Supports, resources, and training needed for personnel to implement this plan in the current/most likely setting)	• Bimonthly training for all staff • Biweekly training for core staff • Social story development (initiating conversation, maintaining conversation, asking for something) • Purchase social skills curriculum, $100 for all student and staff materials • Specific training for playground staff on supervision skills, scanning the environment, deescalating behavior, and helping peers play together
Generalization (Supports, resources, and training needed for personnel to implement this plan across multiple settings)	• When data indicate 80 percent success begin fading reinforcement by halves • Refresher trainings scheduled as needed • Build in an extra ten minutes each afternoon to practice in different settings
Communicating the Behavior Intervention Plan	The plan will be communicated to the following people (that is, bus driver, clinic aide, school resource officer, etc.)

Person to be contacted:	How contact will be made:	Person responsible for contact:	Date/frequency of contact:
Caregivers	Meeting	School psychologist	Monthly
Playground staff	Ongoing training	Social worker	As needed
Bus driver	Face to face	Classroom teacher	As needed

Who will communicate revisions and updates internally and externally?
The classroom teacher will work with the MDT to make any necessary adjustments to the plan. If changes are made, the team will send an email to all staff with general updates. Core plan implementers will receive additional training. The social worker will update and disseminate laminated one-page plans.

NOTE

1. E. L. Deci, R. Koestner, R. Richard, and M. Richard, "A Meta-Analytic Review of Experiments Examining the Effects of Extrinsic Rewards on Intrinsic Motivation," *Psychological Bulletin* 125, no. 6 (November 1999): 627–68.

Conclusion

A Recipe for a Happy Student

Better than a thousand days of diligent study is one day with a great teacher.

—*Japanese Proverb*

INGREDIENTS

- A heaping portion of challenging behavior
- A collaborative multi-disciplinary team
- A dash of data
- One strong hypothesis
- One function of behavior
- An ounce of prevention
- A fabulous FERB
- A handful of preferred reinforcers
- Gingerly sprinkled generalization strategies

Begin by collecting relevant baseline information. Continue to add data. Throw in the hypothesized function of behavior. Whip in the preventative approaches, replacement behavior, and reinforcement for appropriate behavior. Stir all of the ingredients into a classroom with sound classroom management strategies and continue until all of the ingredients have combined. Continue the process until a happy student is developed.

My first experience with functional behavior assessments and behavior intervention plans was as a classroom aide for a student with severe ADHD and aggressive behavior. I had never worked in a classroom before, let alone with a child that was angry, hurtful, and hyper. I assumed that my loving nature and compassion for children would be enough.

I quickly learned that he needed much more! The school hired a behavior analyst from a local college to work with the staff to develop an FBA/BIP. I admit that I was incredibly skeptical; after all, this student had given me my first black eye, stabbed me in the leg with a pencil, and called me every terrible name in the book.

We met weekly as a team. I was taught data collection strategies and asked to track specific behaviors. We reviewed data and as a team determined that attention was the function of the behavior. The team developed an intervention plan for the aggression and prevention strategies for the classroom.

I was even more skeptical when the behavior analyst told me to practice my happy face. My happy face? She explained that when I said, "good job" I didn't seem that excited. I let her know that I usually wasn't that excited because I had probably argued with the student for twenty minutes before he did what he was supposed to. I left each day extremely exhausted, overwhelmed, and defeated.

But I also took her advice and practiced. I went home and practiced my happy face in the mirror. Happy face with a thumb up. Happy face with two thumbs up. Happy face with a wink and nod. I was determined to find success for this student. There were moments each day when he was successful, so I knew we could do more.

I implemented the plan that the team created. I actively ignored some defined behaviors. I used a crisis plan for dangerous behaviors. I implemented the plan day in and day out.

And one day, while I was sitting on the carpet square with the student, I realized we had been playing uninterrupted for nearly ten minutes. There was no crying, no yelling, and no hitting. There was just calm.

I went home that day in tears. I went home that day and realized that the plan had worked. It wasn't perfect. It required consistency and lots of happy faces, but it worked.

That was more than twenty years ago. I still have the assessment and intervention plan in a binder stored away. After hundreds of students and thousands of FBA/BIPS, that plan is the one that taught me that behavior can change. Even the most powerful, most challenging, or most annoying behavior can be improved.

The FBA/BIP process is not about the compliance of finding students eligible for special education, nor is it a ticket out of the general education classroom door. For the student that I first worked with, the FBA and BIP are what made it so the student could mainstream regularly with his general education peers. The process of the FBA and BIP are what created the environment for him to thrive and succeed.

Like making your favorite meal, it requires that the right ingredients are included. It requires that the recipe be followed. And, like a great recipe, you will learn when you can add an extra dash of data or a pinch of prevention.

With all of the ingredients in this book, you have the recipe for success. You have the recipe for a happy student. You are the chef of success!

Appendix A

Blank Functional Behavior Assessment

Functional Behavior Assessment	
Student Name: Teacher Name: Initial Date:	
Description of the Target Behavior (as described and/or observed by classroom staff)	
Operational Definition of Target Behavior (should include all elements necessary)	
Setting(s) in which the Target Behavior occurs most often (as described and/or observed by classroom staff)	☐Classroom ☐Hallway ☐Specials/Electives ☐Playground/Parking Lot ☐ Gym ☐Cafeteria ☐Office Areas ☐Bus/Transportation ☐Transitions (between activities, between subject areas, between classes, etc.) ☐Unknown ☐Other- Describe
Anecdotal Report	Teacher Interview: Student Interview: Parent Interview: Other:
Observation and Data Collection Summary	Observation 1 Date/Time: Setting: Summary of Observation Information: Observation 2 Date/Time: Setting: Summary of Observation Information: Observation 3 Date/Time: Setting: Summary of Observation Information:

	ABC Data Review/Summary:
Data Collection Method and Graphs	

Data Collection Tools
• ABC Data
• Can't Do v. Won't Do
• Event Recording, Frequency
    o Exact
    o Whole Interval
    o Partial Interval
• Duration
• Latency
• Intensity
	Description of Data Collection Method Used (Baseline data should be graphed and inserted in this area):

Function of Behavior	
Function of Behavior (as determined by data, record review, interviews, hypothesis statement) Tools to assist with Function determination: • Competing Behaviors Pathway • FAST • MAS • QABF	Attention (Adults) ☐ Attention (Peers) ☐ Escape/Avoid ☐ Tangible ☐ Sensory ☐
Hypothesis Statement or Target Behavior	When (setting/environmental factors) _____ the student will (target behavior) _____ in order to gain (function) _____ as supported by (data utilized) _____ .
Behavior Intervention Plan	
Sources of Information: (List sources of information used in FBA, both formal and informal, to develop this plan)	
Strength Based Profile: (Identify skills and interests, positive relationships, pro-social behaviors, family and community supports, and other protective factors)	
Functional Behavioral Assessment (FBA) Summary Statement: (Describe specific problem behavior and summary/hypothesis statement from FBA)	

Functionally Equivalent Replacement Behavior: (Behavior that provides the same functional outcome in a socially appropriate manner)	
Setting Event Strategies (Reduce impact of setting events)	**Antecedent Strategies** (Decrease likelihood that behavior will occur)
•	•
Evaluation and Continuous Progress Monitoring Method:	Person Responsible:
FERB Behavior Strategies Increase the likelihood that the appropriate replacement behavior will occur through instruction	
•	
Reinforcement of the FERB Strategies (Consequence)	
•	
Criterion for Success:	Follow-up Meeting Date:
Contextual Fit (Supports, resources and training needed for personnel to implement this plan in the current/most likely setting)	
Generalization (Supports, resources and training needed for personnel to implement this plan across multiple settings)	
Communicating the Behavior Intervention Plan	

Person to be contacted:	How contact will be made:	Person responsible for contact:	Date/Frequency of contact:

Who will communicate revisions and updates internally and externally?

Appendix B

Sonya's Functional
Behavior Assessment

Functional Behavior Assessment

Student Name: Sonya M.
Teacher Name: J. Sage
Initial Date: October 11, 2018
Description of the Target Behavior (as described and/or observed by classroom staff)
Hitting other students, aggression, not playing with others
Operational Definition of Target Behavior (should include all elements necessary)
Sonya's hitting behavior is defined as a hit that makes physical contact with a person or object using an open hand, closed fist, or any or all parts of the hand connecting with the person or object. The hitting may or may not leave a mark. The hitting may also include other parts of the arm connecting with the person or object. The hitting behavior occurs nearly 6 times per week during recess. The hitting does not leave a mark on the other person and each hit lasts only a second or two.

Setting(s) in which the Target Behavior occurs most often (as described and/or observed by classroom staff)	☒Classroom ☒Hallway ☐Specials/Electives ☒Playground/Parking Lot ☐ Gym ☐Cafeteria ☐Office Areas ☐Bus/Transportation ☒Transitions (between activities, between subject areas, between classes, etc.) ☐Unknown ☐Other- Describe
Anecdotal Report	**Teacher Interview:** • How often do you believe, or have you observed, the hitting behavior occurs? *I have seen hitting several times on the playground but I have heard other students mention that they have seen her hit friends. My partner teacher also mentioned one day that she had seen Sonya lash out at a classmate.* • Does hitting only occur during recess or has it been reported or observed in other locations? *I think it happens during times or in places where there is less structure. I see other behaviors in the classroom during transitions and when all the*

| | students are together it can be chaotic and overwhelming. It is loud and a bit over-stimulating. My partner teacher mentioned that she saw Sonya hit another student in the hallway.
• What happens right after the hitting? How do adults respond? How do the other students and the victim respond? *In the instances that I have seen the hitting, the student that was hit began crying and yelling, the other students around Sonya got mad at her and told her to stop and the adult that was monitoring during recess immediately went over and talked to Sonya about how hitting is bad and made her apologize. I don't have much information about the other instances. My partner teacher might be able to share details of what she saw.*
• What strategies have been tried to stop the hitting? *Well, after Sonya has hit, she has had to apologize, she has been removed from the situation, she has lost privileges, and she has gotten a phone call home.*
• How do you feel those have worked? *I'm not sure. The apology made the other student feel better temporarily. But I think that Sonya continues to become more aggressive. While she isn't hitting students in the classroom that I have seen, she has been more confrontational, argumentative, and emotional. I can see her physically lashing out at students in the classroom if something isn't done.*
• Are there other behaviors that you are concerned about? *Hitting is pretty extreme but she also is very disruptive in the class. She wanders around the classroom, she fidgets a lot, and she has a hard time sitting still. And, like I mentioned she has become more emotional which can also be disruptive.*
• Where do those most often and least often occur? *Well it happens in the classroom but the more I think about it, it starts after we have transitions. When we move from one activity to the next. That is probably most often. Sometimes it happens when the students are doing independent work. She will try to get me to spend more time with her.*
• What strategies have been tried to decrease those behaviors? *I feel like I've tried everything. I have* |

moved her seat. I have tried to comfort her. I have used time out, a lot. She has lost privileges. Most often, I think I try to redirect her and get her to refocus. I noticed that when I work with her more one on one, she seems fine.

- What has worked and not worked? *Most of the strategies I described really haven't made it better and I can't work with her one on one all day long. The other students need me too. The only other thing that has worked in the past was going to visit her favorite specials teacher Mrs. Davidson. She loves her! I had her go there one day when she couldn't handle being in my class anymore and she came back after 45 minutes like a different child.*

- Is there any other information that you feel would help to create a plan that you will be implementing? *I just know that I'm exhausted. It is hard trying to focus on Sonya and her needs while also helping everyone else. I need to be able to teach and I most certainly don't want other students to be fearful or scared that they'll be hit or hurt. I've already had two other parents contact me with their concerns.*

Student Interview:
- Do you feel happy at school? *Yah. For the most part. Sometimes I get angry at people because I don't get my way.*
- Do you have friends? *Yes. Some days we don't get along but they are my friends still.*
- Is there anything that you are having trouble with? *When I get angry I want my teacher to help me and sometimes she doesn't.*
- What helps to make you feel happy at school? *My teacher. I like to draw. I wish we could have alpacas in class.*
- If you could change anything, what would it be? *Nothing.*

Parent Interview:
- Have you seen this challenging behavior occur anywhere else but school? *She is absolutely not allowed to hit in our house. I don't know why this is happening at school but she gets along with her two brothers and has neighborhood friends. I*

	have never seen her be violent toward them. She will have tantrums and get really emotional sometimes if she doesn't get her way but I just figured that was her age. • What strategies do you use to decrease challenging behavior(s)? *If she gets in trouble at home we put her in time out, she has to apologize, she loses her allowance for the week. We also use a chart for her to earn that allowance. She has specific tasks she has to accomplish each week. She likes that because she gets to help me around the house.* • What are the sleeping and eating patterns at home? *Okay. There are times that she doesn't sleep well and I know she is cranky and tired but I have to send her to school because I have to work. She eats fine. She is a growing girl.* • Are there any medical issues that may have an impact at school? *She goes the doctor regularly and for things like the cold or flu but she doesn't have any issues. Her father has a temper and they once said that it might be something mental or medical, like ADHD or something.* • What does the student say about school at the end of the day? *Most of the time she doesn't say much. Occasionally she has mentioned that she got into a fight with her friends. I never thought that meant hitting.* • What are the student's favorite things to do or people to see? *She loves her aunt to death and she likes when we get to grocery shopping together or go to the store.*
Observation and Data Collection Summary	**Observation 1** Date/Time: 11/16 Setting: Transition from Class to Outside Summary of Observation Information: *Sonya was the line leader. A number of students complained. The teacher and adult volunteer in the classroom did not notice the disturbance until Sonya had pushed a student. The process to line up was a bit chaotic. There was also a fire alarm during the morning prior to this observation.* **Observation 2**

	Date/Time: 12/1 Setting: Classroom Summary of Observation Information: *Sonya appeared to be sleeping when the observation began. The class was instructed to build a model of a building out of popsicle sticks. Sonya was talking loudly with classmates. Classmates did not appear to engage with Sonya. Sonya spent approximately five minutes wandering around the classroom. The teacher pulled Sonya aside and spoke with her about getting along with classmates.* **Observation 3** Date/Time: 12/3 Setting: Outside Summary of Observation Information: *Sonya was playing on the outside equipment. Classmates were not interacting with her. Sonya appeared to become angry or frustrated—she clenched her fists, her face became red, she began to vocalize loudly. One classmate told the adult nearby and that adult went and spoke with Sonya about how to play with others.* **ABC Data Review/Summary:** *Most often when Sonya is approached or in close proximity with a classmate there is hitting behavior, which is most often followed by a reaction from a peer and a reprimand from the teacher.*

Data Collection Method and Graphs
 	
Data Collection Tools
• ABC Data
• Can't Do v. Won't Do
• Event Recording, Frequency
    ○ Exact
    ○ Whole Interval
    ○ Partial Interval
• Duration
• Latency
• Intensity
	Description of Data Collection Method Used (Baseline data should be graphed and inserted in this area):
	
	Data included ABC data recording over several observations; tally of hitting behavior
	
	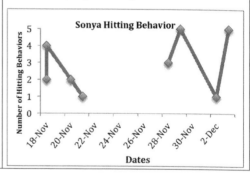

Function of Behavior (as determined by data, record review, interviews, hypothesis statement) Tools to assist with Function determination: • Competing Behaviors Pathway • FAST • MAS • QABF	Attention (Adults) ☐ Attention (Peers) ☒ Escape/Avoid ☐ Tangible ☐ Sensory ☐
Hypothesis Statement or Target Behavior	When Sonya is on the playground or in unstructured settings with few adults she will hit other students in order to gain attention from her peers as supported by ABC, baseline, and MAS/FAST data.

Behavior Intervention Plan
Sources of Information: (List sources of information used in FBA, both formal and informal, to develop this plan) Anecdotal teacher information; ABC data; Interviews; Frequency data; MAS and FAST
Strength Based Profile (Identify skills and interests, positive relationships, pro-social behaviors, family and community supports, and other protective factors) *Sonya is full of life and energy. She has a strong desire to learn and interact with her peers. She loves her family and speaks of them often. She enjoys drawing, coloring and crafting and often incorporates her two dogs into her art. Sonya thrives in a classroom that is structured and rule-bound. She forms immediate bonds with adults. Sonya is able to participate in all classroom activities. Sonya enjoys leadership roles and being 'the princess'.*
Functional Behavioral Assessment (FBA) Summary Statement (Describe specific problem behavior and summary/hypothesis statement from FBA) When Sonya is on the playground or in unstructured settings with few adults she will hit other students in order to gain attention from her peers as supported by ABC, baseline, and MAS/FAST data.

Functionally Equivalent Replacement Behavior
(Behavior that provides the same functional outcome in a socially appropriate manner)

• Request access to preferred items using age appropriate language	
Setting Event Strategies (Reduce impact of setting events)	**Antecedent Strategies** (Decrease likelihood that behavior will occur)
• Social Story • Quiet bell work • Social skills practice • Mid morning rest	• Teach peers to share • Teach Sonya to request items or playtime with peers • Schedule peer to peer playtime during recess- organize play

FERB Behavior Strategies **Increase the likelihood that the appropriate replacement behavior will occur through instruction**
• Sonya will be taught to initiate conversation with peers • Staff will utilize a peer to peer social skills program • Sonya will have twenty minutes each morning to read a Social Story about peer to peer interaction • After the Social Story, Sonya will choose one peer to practice with for ten minutes • On the playground, Sonya will be partnered with a student buddy who will help to initiate peer to peer conversation • Sonya may only utilize equipment or toys that she has asked appropriately for, classmates have been taught to say, 'not right now, Sonya, please ask nicely.' • Sonya, will be prompted/reminded to initiate conversation by saying, 'hi, I'm interested in that, can I play?' or 'hi, I'd like to join, may I?'

Reinforcement of the FERB Strategies (Consequence)
• When Sonya appropriately initiates conversation with her classmates she can earn a sticker • Each sticker is worth one minute of additional freetime with a preferred peer at the end of the day • Sonya also earns a bonus sticker each morning for completing her Social Story practice appropriately • She can earn up to ten stickers a day (based on baseline data)

Evaluation and Continuous Progress Monitoring Method: Frequency data Monitored weekly by core MDT Share with family monthly	**Person Responsible:** Data collection- classroom teacher Data graphing- social worker Weekly meetings- classroom teacher Monthly meetings- school psychologist

Criterion for Success: Sonya will interact with peers and maintain appropriate conversation without physical or verbal aggression 90% of all observed occasions within eight weeks.	Follow-up Meeting Date: January 7, 2019
Contextual Fit (Supports, resources and training needed for personnel to implement this plan in the current/most likely setting)	• Bi-monthly training for all staff • Bi-weekly training for core staff • Social Story development (initiating conversation, maintaining conversation, asking for something) • Purchase Social Skills curriculum $100 for all student and staff materials • Specific training for playground staff on supervision skills, scanning the environment, de-escalating behavior and helping peers play together
Generalization (Supports, resources and training needed for personnel to implement this plan across multiple settings)	• When data indicate 80% success begin fading reinforcement by halves • Refresher trainings scheduled as needed • Build in an extra ten minutes each afternoon to practice in different settings
Communicating the Behavior Intervention Plan	The plan will be communicated to the following people (i.e. bus driver, clinic aid, school resource officer, etc.)

Person to be contacted:	How contact will be made:	Person responsible for contact:	Date/Frequency of contact:
Caregivers	Meeting	School psychologist	Monthly
Playground staff	Ongoing training	Social Worker	As needed
Bus Driver	Face to face	Classroom teacher	As needed

Who will communicate revisions and updates internally and externally?

The classroom teacher will work with the MDT to make any necessary adjustments to the plan. If changes are made the team will send an email to all staff with general updates. Core plan implementers will receive additional training. The social worker will update and disseminate laminated one page plans

Appendix C

Murray's Functional
Behavior Assessment

Functional Behavior Assessment	
Student Name: Murray S. **Teacher Name:** J. Sage (homeroom)	
Initial Date: 1/22/18	
Description of the Target Behavior (as described and/or observed by classroom staff) Joking with classmates, goofing off, not paying attention in class, mouthing back to teachers and adults, being disrespectful	
Operational Definition of Target Behavior (should include all elements necessary) Murray's mouthing off behavior is defined as vocalizations that are unrelated to instruction or activities. Vocalizations may be inappropriate based on school rules and policies, may include threats or harmful terms. Vocalizations may or may not be directly addressed to another student or staff member. Vocalizations occur up to 15 times during a 50-minute class period and are above a whisper level. Vocalizations can be heard throughout the classroom environment.	
Setting(s) in which the Target Behavior occurs most often (as described and/or observed by classroom staff)	☒Classroom ☐Hallway ☒Specials/Electives ☐Playground/Parking Lot ☐Gym ☐Cafeteria ☐Office Areas ☐Bus/Transportation ☐Transitions (between activities, between subject areas, between classes, etc.) ☐Unknown ☐Other- Describe
Anecdotal Report	**Teacher Interview:** • How often do you believe, or have you observed, the behavior occurring? *It feels like it happens anytime Murray is around his friends. He seems to like when they all laugh at his jokes or when he goofs off in class.* • What happens right after the behavior? How do adults respond? *His friends usually laugh and high five him. I try to ignore it but sometimes his goofing off can be dangerous like when he gets on top of*

| | *chairs or desks, then I have to yell at him to get down. He'll also leave the classroom frequently or show up late to class.*
• What strategies have been tried to stop the behavior? *I have tried giving him detention. I've tried calling his family. I've tried sending him to another classroom. I've tried talking to him. Nothing seems to help.*
• Where do those most often and least often occur? *I see it in the classroom and in the hallways. Anytime he has an audience.*
• What has worked and not worked? *One time his best friend in the class was gone for a week, it was quiet that week. It was almost like Murray needed a break and he could focus without trying to impress everyone.*

Student Interview:
• Do you feel happy at school? *Sometimes.*
• Do you have friends? *I do have a couple good friends, I think. But not like I had in my old neighborhood. These kids are from all over and I only see them or hang with them at school because they live too far from me.*
• Is there anything that you are having trouble with? *I'm not getting good grades.*
• If you could change anything, what would it be? *I wish I was really good at math and reading so I could get Mrs. Sage to tell me 'good job' all the time.*

Parent Interview:
• Have you seen this challenging behavior occur anywhere else but school? *No. Murray is very well behaved at home. There are some days when he is a bit cranky because* |

	he didn't sleep well but he minds his manners with us. • What strategies do you use to decrease challenging behavior(s)? *If he ever is disrespectful he has to go to his room and he can't play with his video games or his little brothers and sisters.* • Are there any medical issues that may have an impact at school? *Not that we know of.* • What are the student's favorite things to do or people to see? *He likes to visit his parents and he loves showing people new magic tricks. Oh, and ice cream. He loves ice cream*
Observation and Data Collection Summary	**Observation 1** Date/Time: 1.22.18 Setting: Classroom Summary of Observation Information: Murray was observed during 3rd period English. He was supposed to begin with bellwork and transition to a group project on Shakespeare. He began the class in his assigned seat but did not engage in the bellwork. When he transitioned he quickly went and sat with his friend's at a group that he was not assigned to. When told to move to his group table he shoved his books off the table and left the room. **Observation 2** Date/Time: 1.24.18 Setting: Hallway Summary of Observation Information: Murray was observed walking in the hallway between 2nd and 3rd periods. He was observed waiting by a friends locker, then using the restroom twice, and going to the other end of the hallway to another friend's locker. He was eight minutes tardy to his 3rd period English class. **Observation 3** Date/Time: 1.28.18 Setting: Classroom

	Summary of Observation Information: Murray was observed in his Art elective. His friend Jo is in that class. They sat next to each other and Murray completed the art project early. He was asked to help a friend by the Art teacher and he chose to assist Mary. They worked well together. ABC Data Review/Summary: Antecedents are primarily the presence of Murray's friends or classmates. The Behavior is engaging in inappropriate vocalizations. The most common consequence is he leaves the area out of frustration or is told to leave.

Data Collection Method and Graphs	

Data Collection Tools
• ABC Data
• Can't Do v. Won't Do
• Event Recording, Frequency
    o Exact
    o Whole Interval
    o Partial Interval
• Duration
• Latency
• Intensity
	Description of Data Collection Method Used (Baseline data should be graphed and inserted in this area):
	
	Data included frequency, ABC data
	
	Murray Verbalization and Wandering

Function of Behavior	
Function of Behavior (as determined by data, record review, interviews, hypothesis statement) Tools to assist with Function determination: • Competing Behaviors Pathway • FAST • MAS • QABF	Attention (Adults) ☐ Attention (Peers) ☐ Escape/Avoid ☒ Tangible ☐ Sensory ☐
Hypothesis Statement or Target Behavior	When (setting/environmental factors) in the classroom or hallway the student will (target behavior) engage in inappropriate

	vocalizations (mouthing off, telling jokes) in order to gain (function) escape/avoidance as supported by (data utilized) ABC and frequency data.

Behavior Intervention Plan

Sources of Information:
(List sources of information used in FBA, both formal and informal, to develop this plan)

Anecdotal teacher information; ABC data; Interviews; Frequency data; MAS and QABF

Strength Based Profile:
(Identify skills and interests, positive relationships, pro-social behaviors, family and community supports, and other protective factors)

Murray has strong connections to his peers. He believes strongly in loyalty and friendship. He has strong will toward independence and prefers to learn through experience. Murray is creative and energetic. He performs magic and is a skilled skateboarder. Murray has developed strong bonds to specific family members and will incorporate childhood memories into his writing. He is imaginative and a big picture thinker. Murray prefers opportunities to work with partners and have collaborative projects.

Functional Behavioral Assessment (FBA) Summary Statement:
(Describe specific problem behavior and summary/hypothesis statement from FBA)

When (setting/environmental factors) in the classroom or hallway the student will (target behavior) engage in inappropriate vocalizations (mouthing off, telling jokes) in order to gain (function) escape/avoidance as supported by (data utilized) ABC and frequency data.

Functionally Equivalent Replacement Behavior:
(Behavior that provides the same functional outcome in a socially appropriate manner)
- Murray will request a two-minute time away when he feels anxious, upset, or frustrated

Setting Event Strategies (Reduce impact of setting events)	Antecedent Strategies (Decrease likelihood that behavior will occur)
• Sit Murray in a desk near the teacher • Sit Murray next to strong class models • Use a timer on Murray's phone to indicate transitions, start and end times	• Teach peers to ignore • Teach Murray to request a 'hold' when beginning a new task and allow for time to process new information • Schedule several breaks between class activities (if possible)

FERB Behavior Strategies
Increase the likelihood that the appropriate replacement behavior will occur through instruction

- Teach Murray to request a 'time away'
- Teach Murray to self monitor the time using a two minute stop watch on his phone
- Have Murray's peers welcome him back after two minutes
- Assign a 'catch up' buddy to help Murray get on track with task/activity

Reinforcement of the FERB Strategies (Consequence)
<ul><li>When Murray requests a 'time away' and returns to his task and begins he will earn a Dragon Dollar</li><li>Each Dragon Dollar is worth 30 seconds of free time</li><li>Dragon Dollars can be exchanged for free time or no homework at the end of each day</li><li>Allow for a Magic Minute at the end of classes when Murray has time (after completing all work)</li></ul>

Evaluation and Continuous Progress Monitoring Method: Frequency data Monitored weekly by core MDT Share with family weekly	**Person Responsible:** Data collection- classroom teachers Data graphing- homeroom teacher Weekly meetings- social worker Monthly meetings- school psychologist
Criterion for Success: Murray will request a 'time away' break and return from the breaks without mouthing off or joking around 80% of all observed occasions within the first three weeks.	**Follow-up Meeting Date:** 2.14.18
Contextual Fit (Supports, resources and training needed for personnel to implement this plan in the current/most likely setting)	<ul><li>Initial staff training</li><li>Peer training</li><li>Programming Murray's phone to timers, sync with school schedule</li><li>Purchase magic kit as reward</li><li>Print additional Dragon Dollars</li></ul>
Generalization (Supports, resources and training needed for personnel to implement this plan across multiple settings)	<ul><li>When data indicate 90% success begin fading reinforcement by halves</li><li>Refresher trainings scheduled as needed</li><li>Build in an extra ten minutes each afternoon to practice in different settings</li></ul>
Communicating the Behavior Intervention Plan	The plan will be communicated to the following people (i.e. additional teachers, hallway monitors, office staff, school resource officer, etc.)

Person to be contacted:	How contact will be made:	Person responsible for contact:	Date/Frequency of contact:
Family	Meetings	Homeroom teacher	Weekly
All classroom teachers	Ongoing training	Homeroom teacher	Daily
Family social worker	Phone contact	Social Worker	As needed

Who will communicate revisions and updates internally and externally?
The homeroom teacher will work with the MDT to make any necessary adjustments to the plan. If changes are made the team will send an email to all staff with general updates. Core plan implementers will receive additional training. The homeroom teacher will update and disseminate laminated one page plans.

Index

About the Author

Dr. Jenna Sage has worked in multiple capacities in the field of education for over twenty years. She began as a classroom paraprofessional for a student with special needs. She then went on to graduate with a Bachelor of Science in Psychology with a specialization in Behavior Analysis, an MEd in Special Education, a PhD in Special Education with a focus on systems change for students with disabilities, as well as a certification in Applied Behavior Analysis and certification as a professional and life coach.

As a consultant, speaker, and writer, Jenna has written several published articles, the focus of which have been practical strategies for teachers. She has co-authored a chapter in an edited textbook on Positive Behavioral Supports. She has presented at local, national, and international conferences on topics including behavior supports, classroom management, dropout prevention, and supporting students with disabilities. She has also worked with a number of school districts on utilizing effective systems change processes to support ongoing implementation and sustainability of programs. Her previous book, *Happy Class: The Practical Guide to Classroom Management*, is a teacher's manual for creating safe and happy classrooms for students and staff.

As an instructor at the college level, Dr. Sage works with preservice and current educators to hone their skills in applied behavior analysis, functional behavioral plans, positive behavior supports, integrating students with special needs into general education classrooms, and collaboration and consultation skills. Dr. Sage also contributes to the field of education as a Dean of Online Programs for an allied health care school.

Her most important contribution to education, however, has been as a student. Dr. Sage considers herself a high school pushout. She was a student that silently began disengaging from school as early as first grade. Dr. Sage has a deep passion and understanding for education from the student, teacher, and administrator perspectives and through the lens of a researcher and lifelong learner.

Made in the USA
Middletown, DE
18 January 2022

59064166R00080